The COVID-19 Test: Church or God?

Religion or Relationship?

Rosemarie Downer, Ph.D.

The Covid Test: Church or God?
Religion or Relationship?

by

Rosemarie Downer, Ph.D.

Copyright © 2021

ISBN: 9798777363138

Independently Published

Scripture quotations marked (KJV) are taken from the Holy Bible, King James Version, Cambridge, 1769. Used by permission. All rights reserved.

Scripture quotations marked (NIV) are taken from the Holy Bible, New International Version®, NIV®. Copyright © 1973, 1978, 1984 by Biblica, Inc.™ Used by permission of Zondervan. All rights reserved worldwide. www.zondervan.com

Scripture quotations marked (NLT) are taken from the Holy Bible, New Living Translation, Tyndale House Publishers, 2004 by Tyndale House Publishers, Wheaton, Ill

DEDICATION

This book is dedicated to my beloved mom who taught me many virtues that have made me who I am today. Above all, Mom taught me to love the Lord with all my heart simply by living a life of faith. My mom's life was the sermon that beckoned me to Christ, and thanks be to God, I answered the call. Mom did not verbally teach me how to pray, but many mornings I heard her praying in the living room while I laid in bed. I learned from her that prayer was everything. I learned the worth of the hymns by watching her sing them over the kitchen sink while weeping in worship.

Some of the principles Mom taught and by which I live my life are never give up, don't be afraid of hard work, only your best is good enough, live beneath your means, fear no man, speak up for yourself, stand your ground, get your own, buy your own house, don't rent, and depend on no one.

Mom, you were a woman of principle, my example and my role model. I aspire to be like you in many ways. Thank you for living a life of faith in Christ that led me to give my life to the Lord. Thank you for the many life-lessons you have taught me in word and in deed. I love you more than words can tell!

FOREWORD

I've always had a keen interest in and have studied eschatology. Therefore, I expect wars, natural disasters, and certainly the imminent return of Christ. But not COVID-17, 18 or 19... no!

I recall canceling one of my trips to Nigeria during the Ebola virus health scare and, due to the rise in the swine flu, being quarantined in a hospital as a precautionary measure after a mission trip from Brazil. But I have never seen or experienced anything like the COVID-19 pandemic. I did not expect anything like this to happen during my lifetime. This disease has significantly impacted every aspect of our lives and has forced many of us to seriously evaluate our relationship with God. Our inability to attend church in person should not have affected our allegiance to the God we serve. However, what we have seen throughout the pandemic has been quite revealing.

In the beginning of the pandemic, most people were unsure about the idea of a virtual church and how it would shape their relationship not only with their fellow brothers and sisters in Christ but with God. Virtual church? What is that? How can I have meaningful worship in my living room? Would God accept my sacrifice of praise via Zoom? Can I stay home for 12 months participating in online services without entering the physical temple and still have an authentic relationship with God? The answer to these questions will depend on whether one is in a religion or a relationship with God.

The COVID-19 Test: Church or God? will help us understand how the unintended consequences of COVID-19 affected personal relationships with God and the unimaginable shift of church culture and church life. That is why I am grateful for this book. In this important and thought-provoking book, Rosemarie Downer sounds the alarm, engages readers in a serious dialogue on how our relationship with God matters beyond mere church attendance, and challenges us to reimagine personal connectivity with God.

It is time to hit the reset button. It is time to get grounded. A careful line must be drawn so that, while we hold true to individualism, our relationship with God does not wane because in-person, corporate worship halted for nearly a year or more. We are now living in a changed world, and we need a changed outlook on the difference between religion and our relationship with God. We must allow this book to awaken us to the new realities we face in this world. If you are serious about staying grounded in your faith during times of crisis, this is a very direct and soul-searching book to read.

Our relationship with God is personal and must be portrayed that way. During the periods of social isolation, we were not isolated from God. Our personal relationship with Him should not be negatively affected because we couldn't be in a sanctuary. A meaningful relationship with God is not just about attending church services but is more about personal practice, a lifestyle of daily reading and meditation on the Word of God, a faith-filled prayer life, and consistent public affirmation of our faith.

It is not just that this virus killed over one million people worldwide thus far. It is also that the loyalty of millions of Christians and their relationship with God was called into question. So, every pastor, seminary student, casual churchgoer, and even those who have lost faith during the pandemic and have decided not to come back to church should read this book. This book is the right antidote to inoculate us from further decay in our relationship with God.

Gilford T. Monrose
Lead Pastor, Historic Mt. Zion Church of God 7th Day, Brooklyn, NY

TABLE OF CONTENTS

> Most Christians today refer to church in an entirely different way than Christ our Savior did. Some make a faint distinction between church and the God they claim to worship, but there is a significant difference between church and the God we serve.

> The COVID-19 pandemic led to the temporary cessation of all corporate worship gathering, which certainly has had an impact on church leaders and congregants. How did this unexpected and drastic action affect church leaders?

> The church is made up of people who are at different levels of intimacy in their relationship with the Lord. How did the COVID-19 temporary cessation of corporate worship services affect these individuals and why?

> Many Christians have walked with the Lord for years and have become accustomed to Christendom and its operations. Can this level of familiarity with church cause stagnation in one's walk with the Lord?

> Idolatry is pervasive today like never before. The broad notion today is that right is wrong and wrong is right, and we tend to settle for good instead of aiming for the best. Many Christians have succumbed to this culture and have created idols that

have replaced God and don't seem to know it. These idols are disguised but are damaging just the same.

Church is good, but God is better. Church can be exciting, but God is even more exciting. Many Christians have displaced affection, be it on church or other icons and systems of the world and seem to be totally unaware of it.

Christ is the husband, and the church is the bride. He is married to the church corporately and to us as individuals. As believers, we are in a marriage relationship with Christ which must be nurtured by our deepest love for Him.

Our husband, the Lord and Savior is jealous of us. He wants our complete devotion. He must be the Lord of our lives. He must be first in our lives. His name is Jealous.

INTRODUCTION

A Christian is one who believes in Jesus Christ and follows His teachings. Usually, they hold membership in a local Christian church. As of 2020, approximately 31 percent of the world, well over two billion people, reported that they are Christians.

Christianity is the leading religion in the world. Therefore, every weekend, millions of people stop what they are doing to attend church. Some dress up more than they do for any other day of the week, and nowadays, some go in casual attire. Either way, millions do the minimum of what is expected of a Christian — weekly church attendance. Often, the opportunity to attend mid-week Bible studies and prayer meetings are available. So, attending church services is a significant obligation of a Christian, and doing so is supported by Scripture. We are told in Hebrews 10:25 not to forsake the assembling of the saints together.

Without doubt, church attendance is important. Scripture supports it, but I contend that church gatherings and events should not supersede the God of the church. There is danger in placing too much emphasis on church attendance or church involvement. We, the followers of Christ, must choose God over church, but for too many, church has become their life, while for another set, church gatherings are not nearly as important as they should be. Church should be one element of our walk with Christ; it should not define our walk. There is grave danger in making church the central focus of our lives. Likewise, there is danger in minimizing its value.

Those who minimize or blatantly dismiss the importance of church attendance are likely inconsistent in attending church and are mostly uninvolved with church ministries. With the massive availability of online ministries, many believers — especially late generation Z (born 1997 to 2012) and millennials (born 1981 to 1996) — are growing increasingly convinced that setting foot in a church building is not important to one's faith. A 2020 Gallup Poll reported that, for the first time ever, less than half of Americans (47 percent) say they belong to or are members of a local church. We should refer to this number with caution however, because it is possible that this 47 percent include individuals who attend church but are not members of the church they attend.

There is a third group, those for whom church is not so important that it becomes their life and neither do they ignore its importance, but instead, church is a substitute for what is required to establish and maintain a relationship with Christ. So, they attend church services, but that is all they do to nurture their relationship with the Lord.

With the onset of the COVID-19 pandemic in 2020 came the mandate to cease all gatherings, including churches. This book, *The COVID-19 Test: Church or God?*, discusses the impact of this mandate on four groups of church goers:

1. Church Lifers
2. Relationals
3. Supplanters
4. Minimals

The discussion focuses mainly on those who have made church their life (Church Lifers), those who have used church attendance as the substitute for fellowship with Christ their Savior (Supplanters), and those who already saw little value in church attendance and perhaps were already inconsistent and inactive in a local church (Minimals).

The questions remain: How did the COVID-19 lockdown affect these believers? What does the impact of the lockdown say about where they place church and where they place God in their lives? Did any members of these groups of churchgoers emerge from the lockdown God-deficient or were they more spiritually connected? Why would the effect of the lockdown on any believer differ from another believer? *The COVID-19 Test: Church or God?* will engage you in an examination of these and many more questions while providing some thought-provoking answers.

The COVID-19 Test: Church or God? talks about the place that church has taken in the lives of many modern-day Christians. The book addresses some of the dangers of making church far too important in our walk or using church as a substitute for the particularly important personal and private religious practices that are essential to our growth in Christ, and it talks about the risks of eliminating church from our lives.

The book boldly addresses some issues that many do not talk about: spiritual adultery, idolatry, spiritual apathy, lukewarmness, the status quo, and mediocrity. The book also engages in a deep discussion of the relationship our Father and Creator desires to have with us and our role in establishing and maintaining such a relationship with Him.

God wants to have a relationship with us. He is seeking lovers. He is looking for those who pursue His heart, those who seek Him instead of the systems and features we have established to create what we call the church.

Are you seeking to go deeper in the Lord? Do you want a closer walk with the Lord? Do you want to know how to personalize your relationship with Him? Do you know there is more in Him that you have not yet tapped into? Come with me through this discourse of where we as believers in Christ are, how we got there, where our Heavenly Father wants us to be, and how we can get there.

1

WHAT'S THE DIFFERENCE?

Often when people, including Christians, talk about the church, they are thinking solely of a building for public Christian worship, but such a concept could not be any more inaccurate. For example, to say, "I will meet you at church tomorrow before choir rehearsal," is referring to the church as a building. The visible and physical structures in which public worship takes place are houses of worship, but they are not the church, at least not from Christ's perspective.

Keep in mind that the early church did not have specifically designed or set aside buildings in which they gathered for worship. First century Christians endured severe persecution, and as a result, were often forced to meet in secret. They generally met in private homes, but they, the people, was the church, not the places they gathered for worship. It was only later, as an effect of the spread of Christianity, that buildings were set aside and dedicated to a singular purpose of worship — what we call church. The most common things that happen among believers are fellowship, worship, and ministry, and are all conducted by people, not by buildings. Church buildings house these activities; they are not the activities.

Biblically, the church is the bride of Christ. The church is the people that make up the various congregations that serve Jesus Christ as Lord and Savior. The church is universal, meaning it is the entire body of Christ, and it is local, a community of people who love and serve the Lord together. Regardless, the church is not contained in a building. And because the church is the bride of Christ, this body of believers is referred to as female. The church is the bride and Jesus is the groom.

Another erroneous definition that is often attributed to church is the combination of things or events that happen in the building or across church buildings. So, ministry activities, such as missions, worship services, Bible studies, prayer meetings, youth meetings, concerts, conferences, baptisms, the Lord's Supper or Communion, vacation Bible schools, food pantries, and anything else that congregations do are all referred to as church. An example in which this concept of church is used could be: "I'm very involved with church; it keeps me quite busy."

It is these two concepts of church I am referring to when I ask the question, "Church or God?"

Church

All my life I have been totally immersed in church — church activities, ministries, and very frequent church attendance. During childhood, my life constituted of school and church, that was it. When I became of age and got my first part-time job while attending high school, my life expanded to church, school, and work, and it remained that way until in my postgraduate years when I started having a social life and going on vacations and weekend getaways. But even then, church was central to my life.

There is plenty of talk today about religious decline, but church still plays an important role in the lives of many. I believe there are those reading these words that can claim some part of their life was also taken up overwhelmingly by church. Church meets our spiritual, social, and for some, civic needs. It also provides a sense of home and belonging for many. So, what, if anything, is wrong with being deeply immersed in church? To answer this question, we must talk about who we are and whose we are.

Who Are We?

We are followers of Christ, the people of God, the church, His bride. Christ is married to us. He is our husband, and we are His bride. Christ is not the church, and the church is not Christ. Christ is the head of the church, the church is His body, and He

Himself is its Savior. Therefore we — the church, His body — are subject to Christ. So, as the bride of Christ, if we make church, instead of Christ, central in our lives, our affection is misplaced. If our focus is on church, we may come to see this faith-walk called Christianity as being about rituals, ministry, religious practices and ceremonies, and doctrine. If we focus on church, we could be religious, not relational. The Pharisees were religious, and there are many accounts in Scripture of Jesus' stark displeasure with them for this reason.

Ephesians 5:31 (NLT) is a New Testament derivative of Old Testament Genesis 2:24 which says, "*A man leaves his father and mother and is joined to his wife, and the two are united into one.*" Apostle Paul adds in verse 32 (KJV) that "*This is a great mystery: but I speak concerning Christ and the church.*" Marriage is a spiritual depiction and testimony of Christ's relationship to the church.

In a marriage, the wife should see herself in relationship to her husband as the church is to Christ. This is the kind of relationship the Apostle Paul was describing in the scripture referenced above. Jesus established a relationship with His people, the church in the real sense of it. Therefore, our focus must be on Him, not institutional religion.

As believers, if we are not careful, we can become totally immersed in church (or religion) so everything else in our lives pales in comparison and be entirely unaware of it. Undoubtedly, church activities and the obligations of ministry can easily dominate our prayer life, the reading and study of the Word, and private worship and devotion. Church can easily dominate our daily walk with Christ and overshadow the importance of a deep personal relationship with God. And because church is inherently a good thing, we can be churchy or religious while being oblivious to a strained relationship with God, and that is dangerous.

Whose Are We?

Due to the once and for all, sin-bearing, substitutionary death of Jesus Christ, and through our acceptance of Jesus, the Son of God as our Savior, we are God's. We were brought by grace through the blood of Jesus into a faith relationship with God (Romans 5:17, 21; Galatians 1:6; Ephesians 3:2). We were rescued from the kingdom of darkness where Satan, sin, and death reign. We are God's. Jesus bought us with His blood (1 Corinthians 6:20; Galatians 3:13). When a person buys something, it belongs to them. Jesus bought us. We are His. That's whose we are.

We are washed, cleansed, and kept by the blood of Jesus, the Word of God, and the Holy Spirit, and therefore all that hindered a relationship with God has been removed. Believers are described as "in Christ." We are in Him and are of Him. We are heirs and joint heirs with Christ (Romans 8:17), not because of any personal merit or quality, but only because we are united to Christ through faith. We are hidden with Christ in God (Colossians 3:3), and we already possess every spiritual blessing (Ephesians 1:3). We are God's.

Church Immersion

I will address this question in much more detail later in the book, but let me address it briefly here. What, if anything, is wrong with being deeply immersed in church?

It is entirely healthy and should be a basic commitment of every believer to be deeply involved and devoted to their local church. In fact, I believe every member of a local church should find a place to serve in ministry. Whether it is within the church building or outside, there is a place for everyone to serve.

To secure the health of any relationship, it is important that there is reciprocation. The same applies to our relationship with what we refer to as the church. Therefore, members of a church should give to the ministry and should receive from the ministry. This engenders a sense of worth and provides the opportunity for the growth of the individuals and of others. But we must put serving or church in its correct place.

Church becomes a problem when we are drawn to church activities so much so that we put family, parenting responsibilities, marital relationships, and personal care second to church. Church also becomes a problem when we see church involvement and minis-try activities as being central to our pursuit of God. It is a huge problem when we don't know any other way to be a Christian but to be involved with church. This is true whether passive by merely attending church ser-vices or actively by being involved with church minis-tries. Another huge case in which church becomes a problem is when church is the only place we get our spiritual sustenance.

We must put church in its correct place, but where is that place? Where does church fall in our line-up of priorities and commitments? The Bible does not prioritize church or ministry activities, but instead highlights our relationship with God. God obviously comes first: Deuteronomy 6:5 (NLT) says, "*And you must love the Lord your God with all your heart, all your soul, and all your strength.*" All our heart, soul, and strength are to be committed to loving God, not church. We are to make Him — the Person, Jesus Christ — our pri-ority. Church membership, regular church attendance, and ministry work can be expressions of our love for God, but they must not be the way we love God.

If you are married, your spouse comes next to God. A married man is to love his wife as Christ loved the church (Ephesians 5:25). Christ's priority — after obeying and glorifying the Father — was the church, His bride. The line-up of priorities a husband should follow is God first and then his wife. Similarly, wives are to submit to their husbands "as to the Lord"

(Ephesians 5:22). Thus, in a woman's priorities, her husband is second only to God, not church.

Since a husband and wife are one flesh (Ephesians 5:31) and if husbands and wives are second only to God, it is fair to say that children, which are the result of a marriage relationship, should be the next priority. Parents are to raise godly children who will be the next generation of those who love the Lord with all their hearts (Proverbs 22:6; Ephesians 6:4), showing once again that God comes first. All other family relationships should reflect that.

Deuteronomy 5:16 tells us to honor our parents so that we may live a long and full life. No age limit is specified, which leads me to believe that as long as our parents are alive, we should honor them. In contrast, Ephesians 6:1 (NLT) says, "*Children, obey your parents because you belong to the Lord, for this is the right thing to do.*" Here we see the directive being given to children, so there is an age limit to having to obey one's parents. Adult children are not obligated to obey their parents but there is no age limit to honoring them. This gives me reason to put parents as next in the list of priorities after God, spouses, and children (family).

Some assert that the order of priorities should be God, family, God's family, and others. Another group proposes the priorities thus: God and His family, family, and others. I think it is fair to say if one puts God first, they have essentially put God's family first as well. What better way to love God than to love His people? John 13:34 and 1 John 4:11 show us that loving other believers is evidence of our love for God. However, despite the order of things, there is no controversy that God comes first.

So now I am giving you a new commandment: Love each other. Just as I have loved you, you should love each other. – John 13:34, NLT

Dear friends, since God loved us that much, we surely ought to love each other. – 1 John 4:11, NLT

It is important to go back to the Bible verse that tells us to love the Lord with all we have. The verse is Deuteronomy 6:5 (NLT), and it says, "*And you must love the Lord your God with all your heart, all your soul, and all your strength.*" To further look at the difference between church and God, it is worth examining what "love the Lord" really means. This then brings us to the discussion of God.

God

Again, it is especially important to note that in Deuteronomy 6:5, we are called to love the Lord. We have clarified that while Christ is the head of the church, He is not the church, and the church is not Him. Though we cannot separate the church from the Lord, there is a difference between the two. This brings me to the conclusion that the exhortation in Deuteronomy 6:5 is not saying that we should love church. The appeal is specifically to love the Lord Jesus Christ, the one who purchased our salvation with His shed blood.

Loving God is the highest aspiration of mankind or the zenith of fulfillment, not church. If loving church was the goal, then a scriptural command to love church would be our greatest calling. Instead, it's to love God most (Matthew 22:37-40). In His love, we can find fulfillment that no institution, not even our concept of church, can provide.

> *37 Jesus said unto him, Thou shalt love the Lord thy God with all thy heart, and with all thy soul, and with all thy mind. 38 This is the first and great commandment. 39 And the second is like unto it, Thou shalt love thy neighbour as thyself. 40 On these two commandments hang all the law and the prophets.* – Matthew 22:37-40, KJV

God wants us to pursue Him. Now, that does not mean we are not to love the church. We cannot love God in the abstract. In fact, out of our love for God will flow love for the church that is talked about in Hebrews 6:10.

> *For God is not unjust. He will not forget how hard you have worked for him and how you have shown your love to him by caring for other believers, as you still do.* – Hebrews 6:10, NLT

The church that is referenced in Hebrews 6:10 is God's people, "*other believers.*" So, one way to show our love for God is by active love for the church, His people. Note here that church in Hebrews 6:10 does not mean church building, church ministries, ceremonies, or church events and traditions. It means people, other believers. Therefore, it would be conflicting to say we love the Lord but not love the church, meaning God's people.

The call is to love the Lord, and not just love Him casually, but to do so with all our being. Therefore, there must be an internal response to obey Deuteronomy 6:5. The focus is not on the external as it is with loving church, which is defined by church attendance, religious practices and ceremonies, and church ministries. This command demands a heart response. It requires a personal, spiritual relationship with the Lord that is built upon our faith in Him.

John 14:15 (KJV) says, "*If ye love me, keep my commandment.*" And of all His commandments, which is the most important? Of everything God has told us to do, what matters most?

> [29] *And Jesus answered him, The first of all the commandments is, Hear, O Israel; The Lord our God is one Lord:* [30] *And thou shalt love the Lord thy God with all thy heart, and with all thy soul, and with all thy mind, and with all thy strength: this is the first commandment.* [31] *And the second*

is like, namely this, Thou shalt love thy neighbour as thyself. There is none other commandment greater than these. – Mark 12:29-31, KJV

Of everything God has told us to do, what matters most is to love the Lord and, secondly, to love our neighbors as ourselves. "*On these two commandments hang all the law and the prophets*" (Matthew 22:40, KJV). Therefore, everything that God says to us and all that He calls us to do can be summed up in these two things: Love God with all your heart and love your neighbor as yourself. Nothing is more important than that. If we obey these two commands, we automatically obey all the other commands because our love for Christ makes us want to obey everything else He says so that our ways will please Him. This relationship is founded in love alone.

It is utterly reasonable for God to command us to love Him. After all, He first loved us. He sent His only begotten Son to this sin-ridden world to die for our sins. Nothing can measure up to the height and depth of His love for us, and the grief Jesus bore for us will never be known by anyone who walk the face of this earth. This is the price Jesus paid to redeem us from the curse of the law.

Love the Lord with All Your Heart, Soul, and Mind

The Ten Commandments (Exodus 20:3-17; Deuteronomy 5:7-21) lay out what loving God and loving our neighbor look like. None of these commandments refer to loving church.

The first four commands tell us what it means to love God:

1. You shall have no other gods before me (Deuteronomy 5:7)
2. Don't make for yourself an idol of any kind (5:8)
3. Don't take the Lord's name in vain (5:11)
4. Remember the Sabbath day and keep it holy (5:12)

The last six commands tell us what it means to love our neighbor:

5. Honor your father and mother (5:16)
6. Don't murder (5:17)
7. Don't commit adultery (5:18)
8. Don't steal (5:19)
9. Don't give false testimony (5:20)
10. Don't covet what God has given to your neighbor (5:21)

All ten commandments tell us how to live a life that is depicted by love. They tell us how to do what matters most to God our Father. Interestingly, "Deuteronomy" means "second law," meaning it was Moses' retelling of God's laws that were first given in Exodus 20. Chapters 6 to 26 of Deuteronomy is an exposition of the Ten Commandments. Chapters 6 to 18 discuss the first four commandments. They explain what it means for God's people to love Him. These chapters are about worship, love, fear of the Lord, obedience to God and His commandments, keeping from idols and false gods, not following the desires of a stubborn heart, and not abandoning the covenant with God. In summary, these chapters made a call for wholehearted commitment and a call to holy living by loving God, keeping His commandments, and obeying His laws. Chapters 19 to 26 discuss the last six commandments. They explain what it means to love our neighbor as ourselves.

God is love, and He is inviting us into a love relationship with Him, not church and all the church-iness that comes with it. That is why love is the fulfill-ment of the law (Romans 13:10). The Ten Command-ments shows us how to love God's way. If we set our affections on God (Colossians 3:2) and love Him with all our heart, then we will have made a clear distinction between church and God.

2

WHEN THINGS CHANGE

Coronavirus disease 2019 (COVID-19) was declared a pandemic by the World Health Organization (WHO) on March 11, 2020 (World Health Organization, 2020). On March 13, 2020, I was attending a training in Rockville, Maryland, when we got word that hundreds of flights across various airlines were cancelled and that life as usual was coming to a halt because of COVID-19. The instructor, a resident of Toronto, Canada, was rightfully concerned about getting home the next morning. That was the last day for well over a year that I dressed myself in professional attire and left home for a day's work or business venture of any sort. Christians in and beyond the United States that attend weekly religious gatherings suffered the same fate. The weekend before or following was the last for full church gatherings for months.

Undoubtedly, this had a significant impact on the spirituality of church leaders and parishioners alike, but what was the impact on who and why? What did the impact say about their connection with and devotion to God or church?

Church Leaders

The COVID-19 pandemic and related restrictions on gatherings for religious worship in a church building have had a mixed impact on the wellbeing of church leaders. There may be others, but I will talk about four areas related to religious leaders that the COVID-19 lockdown has affected:

1. Spiritual connectivity
2. Family functioning
3. Finances
4. Mental health and wellbeing

We should note that none of these effects are mutually exclusive. For example, an impact on one's finances could have secondary effects on the person's mental health and wellbeing.

Spiritual Connectivity

The lockdown brought an abrupt stop to a basic spiritual practice: church attendance and everything else that comes with it. Religious leaders more than ever before had to quickly adopt alternative means (e.g., telephone, internet) of offering pastoral care and even delivering teachings and sermons, mostly from their homes.[1,2] This significantly contributed to a new meaning for religious participation, community, and the worth and belongingness that church leadership brings.[3] No doubt, the fallout caused a loss of fellowship in the usual manner for all and for some it created spiritual decline.[4]

Being engaged in religious practices with other believers is an inherent boost to one's faith and even more so when you play a key role in preparing for or ensuring the success of such activities. The demand of preparing for these activities alone is a source of spiritual enrichment, and the gathering of believers together further inspires and enriches church leaders.

But the restrictions on public worship challenged the faith of some church leaders in the sense that they found it difficult to prepare and deliver sermons to their congregations. Therefore, in the absence of religious gatherings and potentially a reduction in the demand to prepare for religious activities, there could be spiritual decline.

Another area in which the faith of some was challenged is prayer. An interviewee in a May of 2021 study[5] of the impact of Covid-19 on Christian church leaders shared that his prayer life had not been as it used to be. He added that the degree of prayer he engaged in during the lockdown was not adequate.

The thing he pointed to that had a significant impact on his prayer life was the absence of the encouragement he received when he prayed with others. He shared that when he prayed at home, he got tired, and being confined at home, he often would go to sleep, relax, or even watch television. But when he prayed with other believers, he could pray for hours.

According to the Barna Group,[6] half (51 percent) of church leaders report that it was easy (23 percent very, 28 percent somewhat), while another 49 percent found it difficult (10 percent very, 39 percent somewhat) to prioritize this time for their own spiritual development.

Another area that was affected is preaching. One church leader in the study of the impact of Covid-19 on Christian church leaders raised a concern that, after moving to virtual services, the excitement waned. Even preparation to teach or preach decreased. He added that he learns the Bible when he prepared sermons but that went down drastically during the lockdown.

Another participant had a similar experience. He said pastors regressed during the lockdown because they were not doing all the things they did before the pandemic. He added that pastors regress because, being homebound, they mostly ate and slept.

The church is the central place where members of a local congregation worship, and it is there where scheduled religious practices occur — worship, Word study, and prayer. These regularly scheduled religious activities are done with other believers, and even more so, are the leaders' responsibility for making sure they happen. More so, such activities demand consistency from the organizers. Being removed from that structure could very well cause spiritual decline.

In general, and while this is not optimal, many church leaders give much of themselves to those they serve but do not spend the intimate time needed with the Lord to sustain them spiritually. Most of them are constantly on the go. Meaningful time spent in the Word and in prayer are mostly in preparation to preach or teach, not for personal and spiritual growth. So, there is a high probability that these church leaders will experience spiritual decline when the demand to prepare to minister lessens.

The ban on religious gatherings could take church leaders in either direction. They could see this as a time of reprieve and use the time available to them due to the lockdown for personal and spiritually growth.[7] Others, because of the lack of discipline in spending time in personal devotion, may drift even further away because of the change in routine. There is also the possibility that some church leaders may refocus their time and effort. Meaning, they now become even more deeply immersed in planning and preparing for ministry but on a different platform, which due to its novelty, could require more time.

The halt brought to the church due to the pandemic could be nothing but good for some church leaders as they saw it as a test of faith, and for believers, a test of faith is always an opportunity for spiritual growth. These church leaders are likely to take the change of course as a chance to refocus on the core tenets of their faith, to spend more time in private prayer and devotion, to worry less about building expenses and costly church programming, and focus more on helping the needy and on evangelizing.

Family Functioning

The demands from both family and church have been a source of mental strain for most religious leaders and fulltime pastors.[8,9] Many families with fulltime pastors have grown accustomed to getting what is left of the father's or husband's time after giving first to the ministry. But the restrictions on public gatherings during the pandemic meant that religious leaders had to spend more time with their families at home. Therefore, church leaders could likely experience improved family functioning.

However, at the same time, religious leaders more than ever before had to change the way they deliver services, most of which required methods and skills they have not used before and mostly from the home environment. This could create another layer of family-ministry conflict. Not being in the home due to ministry work was one issue but being in the home and still being drawn away from family because of ministry could be a bigger issue for spouse and children.

The lockdown significantly contributed to framing a new meaning for religious participation, community, belongingness,[10] and family-ministry balance.

Finances

The ban on corporate worship could have significant financial implications now and for the future. For many churches, the absence of people congregating in a church building led to significant reduction in offerings from congregants. In fact, some small churches, due to lack of finances and church members who lost interest, were forced to close their doors.

Michelle Boorstein in an April 24, 2020, Washington Post publication gave an example of a small Mississippi church that faced severe financial strain, especially since they were not in great financial shape before the pandemic. This church suffered a 50 percent reduction in weekly offerings due to the pandemic. She also reported that "About a third of all congregations have no savings, according to the 2018-2019 National Congregations Study. Just 20 percent streamed their services and 48 percent were able to accept donations electronically, the study found, making it more challenging to serve the faithful and gather their donations during the virus shutdown."

The financial impact due to the pandemic was most severe for small churches and the small church in Mississippi that is referenced by Borstein is not an isolated case. About half of U.S. congregations are small (65 members or less). According to Revival Outside the Walls, 68 percent of all evangelical churches in the United States have a congregation with less than 100 people including children and half of those churches have a membership of less than 50.

There is strong suspicion among experts that the coronavirus could reshape the country's religious landscape and permanently close the doors of many small houses of worship. The church is the place where members are inspired and strengthened in their faith-walk, but during the lockdown, members faced closed church buildings and desperate pleas from church leaders for financial support called tithes and offerings. Like never before, people saw multiple ways in which one could give to the church.

Pastors sometimes receive monetary gifts from members of their congregation and even believers who do not attend their church. Believers often see this as a way of blessing those who labor in the ministry. This will more likely happen when there are in-person gatherings. The cessation of religious gatherings brought this means of financial resource to a close.

But despite the bleak financial outlook of churches in the aftermath of the ban on congregate worship, there are churches that reported increased finances. These are the churches that maximized the opportunity to expand their ministries, spoke to the current times and seasons, expanded their reach, engaged all age groups so that none is left behind amid the transformation, and used creative methods to bring the ministry to people in interesting ways.

Mental Health and Wellbeing

Doubtlessly, closing the doors of churches for months on end grossly impacted not only the daily routine, but truthfully, the lives of church leaders. We must note that church leaders are, or perhaps I should say, should be different from the chief executive officer of an IT company, for example. They are or should even differ from the executive director of a nonprofit organization, a community serving organization that meets the needs of the indigent.

Religious leaders do what they do because of the calling of God upon their lives. So, ministry becomes their life. This is why the struggle between family and ministry for so many religious leaders is so great. Because of the place church life or ministry has taken in the lives of church leaders, the cessation of church as usual due to the COVID-19 pandemic was an assault on many church leaders' mental health and wellbeing. For many, the adjustment was demanding and overwhelming.

Religious leaders who are in fulltime ministry, as expected, engage predominantly in ministry related activities daily, most of which involve in-person contact, such as prayer meetings, Bible studies, wedding and funeral ceremonies, and visiting the sick. For many, their ministry defines them. Life without ministry as usual is not the same and is difficult to accept, and doing ministry any other way than the usual is near impossible to accept.

These church leaders want people in the building, and they are discontent if that is not the case. If the main service was 3 hours long before the lockdown, these church leaders find it difficult to adjust; they are the ones who by any means possible try to keep the service at 3 hours, even on a virtual platform. If they customarily preach for an hour before the lockdown, they cannot adjust to the new way of doing things, so they continue to preach for an hour.

These church leaders tend to literally transfer what was happening in their public worship prior to the ban to a virtual platform. They make little to no programming or ministry adjustments to address current issues. They see no need to preach a sermon or teach a lesson that will equip the saints to deal with current issues. If the plan was to preach or teach on XYZ, for example, no matter what's happening, they will preach or teach on XYZ. The pandemic and the shutdown might have been a good time to teach on specific topics that could fortify the saints during such difficult times, but these church leaders who are most wedded to church as usual will not see the need for the adjustment and will give no thought to doing so.

The COVID-19 lockdown challenged many church leaders to pivot on short notice to make accommodations for ministry without personal contact, and that includes churchwide ministry, ministry to and with small groups of people, and personal one-on-one ministries. Many church leaders were not prepared.

Some did not have the skills, resources, or manpower to make the adjustment, and some made minimal adjustment in anticipation of returning to the building. Some went beyond waiting anxiously for the ban to lift; they insisted on and encouraged their members to attend corporate worship even after the government handed down the restriction.

This inflexibility and absence of creativity in service delivery mark the degree to which these church leaders place church over God. So, is it about having church as usual or is it about meeting the spiritual needs of the people and bringing people to Christ? It goes without saying that it should be about meeting the spiritual needs of the people and bringing people to Christ.

To meet people's needs, pastors may need to replace the series they had prepare to teach in the month of April 2020. It would be much more spiritually enriching to teach content that are relevant to the issues being faced at the time. For example, many households dealt with grief and loss of all sorts, and many were depressed, anxious, and fearful, just to name a few issues. It would be timely and relevant to the congregants if pastors addressed those issues. Because the ministry is about meeting the needs of the people, a church leader who has not placed church over God will see the pandemic as an opportune time to reshape the ministry in a way that can speak directly to the needs of the people. They will know that this can be done without being in the building and will make such opportunity the priority over being in the building just to have "church as usual."

Perhaps, if the church did not have cell groups – others call it small groups – before the ban on corporate worship, it could have been time to establish cell groups so that members of the congregation could get more personalized care and teachings. The lack of preparation, the inflexibility, or inability to adjust spiraled into other consequences, mainly I would think, spiritual and financial decline.

According to a study conducted by the Barna Group in 2021, 60,000 churches or 20 percent of all churches in America could close within the next 18 months. The COVID-19 pandemic will bring a fundamental change in the way Americans attend church. This unavoidably triggers a level of stress and concern in religious leaders, especially those of small congregations.

There could be mental health concerns because of the dubiousness of the future of a small church. Pastors who spent their life building the ministry – small or big – may be challenged as they watch it decline during and after the ban on corporate worship. Concerns may rise as they watch the number of people who log on virtually for services decline steadily.

Mental health concerns may surface as they watch relationships that they have developed with their congregants weaken. Community and fellowship among Christians are enriched by in-person, face-to-face interactions. Participants of the study that examined the impact of the COVID-19 pandemic on Christian church leaders share that the inability to interact in person contributed to feelings of despair.

In small churches, the pastor is the person who mostly tends to the needs of the congregation, and as a result, usually develops close relationships with the congregants. Pastors of small congregations usually do not have a ministerial staff to whom they can delegate duties, so they assume most of the workload. Also, though not the healthiest thing to do, many pastors of small congregations have put so much in the work that they find it difficult to delegate even if they have a staff, and if they do delegate, they tend to micro-manage. An abrupt end to church as usual will take a mental toll on these pastors.

Additionally, the COVID-19 virus took a lot of lives, including those of many church members. It added stress as church leaders lost loved ones from their congregations to the virus and at the same time could not perform funeral ceremonies in the usual manner.

Finally, pastoral effectiveness is enhanced by factors such as social comparison and social support from the congregation. Sad to say, but part of the preaching done by some religious leaders is a performance. Therefore, the absence of religious gatherings contributes to boredom and low morale in carrying out their duties.

Furthermore, some religious leaders may experience moral injury when the restrictions do not permit them to fulfill their pastoral duties as they would desire.[11]

Positive Impacts

Despite how bad anything is, there is always some good in it. Good can come out of adversity and that should be the mindset of all believers, especially the leaders. When going through unexpected, painful, or disappointing experiences, if we have the right perspective, we will see the good in it. There are more, but I will discuss three positive impacts of the ban on corporate worship:

1. Increased faith
2. Relief or reduced stress
3. Increased family time

Increased Faith

Increased faith is closely associated with enhanced private, one-on-one time with God and participation and engagement in other personal spiritual development disciplines which can only result in spiritual growth. The ban on religious gatherings could, if not handled well, not only stop regular church attendance but could also stunt personal spiritual development. But a few participants in the COVID-19 church impact study emphasized that the situation afforded them the opportunity to commit more time to building their personal spiritual faith, devotion, and prayer life. One participant admitted, "Spiritually, it hasn't affected me, to be frank, since the COVID came, it has increased my prayer." Another participant stated that she had redirected time previously used for group Bible studies to prayers: "We were not doing that [Bible study], so we are praying more."

Relief or Reduced Stress

Church leaders could very well experience a sense of relief that results from reduction in workload. Indeed, results from the study of church leaders point to that end as some participants described a reduction in their stress level. One participant said, "It [the ban] has made us a little relaxed. It's like you're not so tense, you are not so worried as if, 'Oh I'm not done with this, I'm not done with that, I have to do this, I have to go and see this, I have to attend this engagement.'"

Another participant explained, "The first two weeks it was some kind of relief. Most of us were very tired. So, it's like I was free, let's say you're not so busy." One participant noted that the time afforded the opportunity for developing other interests: "I believe that it's now less stressful than before. We have more time to read, to read other things. We need more time to take care of your body too...exercise, you eat better. For me, I think it is a refreshing time."

Increased Family Time

Family time refers to the time spent with spouse and children or members of one's household. The rigorous demands of pastoral ministry pose a challenge to many fulltime religious leaders to the extent that they sometimes do not spend adequate time with their immediate family, which may result in stress.[12,13] The announcement of the ban on religious gatherings stopped most scheduled church programs and events. Consequently, religious leaders could spend more time with their family members and strengthen existing family ties.

The participants emphasized some of the benefits of the increased family time. One participant described that his family had benefited from being home: "I think while the church is suffering, the family side is prospering. Yeah, the family side is prospering such that now you have time."

Another participant shared, "In fact, you have no place to go, so it has also brought the family together, spending quality time with your family... a lot of time is spent in the house and with my family; it's very, very encouraging and very good."

A specific benefit from the shutdown is improved family cohesion through effective communication and fun activities. Families were afforded time for these enriching activities during the shutdown; time they did not have before. Time that had been dedicated to attending church services had been repurposed for the benefit of married couples and children, as one participant noted:

> Those days [pre-COVID-19 pandemic] when my wife or my spouse returns from work, all she has to do is get something for us to eat. And then to church, [and] I think we come back late around 9 or 9:30 [in the evening]. We have limited time for ourselves, and then the following day in the morning she is gone. So, that has been the old nature, but with this one we get to stay in the house for the whole day, watch TV together, we eat together, we pray together, we talk, we do everything together. So, this one has rather helped improve the family life in terms of communication.

3

A TEST OF VOWS

O ther ways to ask the question, "Church or God?" is, "Religion or relationship?", or "The thing or the Person?" "The thing" refers to church and "the Person" refers to God. Being affiliated with a church is being connected to a house of worship. But choosing God over church is being connected with the Person, Jesus Christ, hence the question: "Religion or relationship?" It is mere religion when our identifier in this faith-walk is the worth we place on church ministries and activities. But when we are in a love relationship with the Lord, we will naturally choose God over church or religion.

Man was made to worship. A. W. Tozer said, "Man's nature indicates that he was created for 3 things: To think, to worship and to work."[14] God created man with the capacity to worship Him. He made man for His pleasure (Isaiah 43:7; Revelation 4:11) and that delight can only be given to God through worship. However, because sin disrupted the plan of God, man's affection that should be rightfully and solely placed on God is displaced on many other things, one of them being "the thing" or church. Although church (the thing) is good, we must not love it more than we love God (the Person).

The worshipper loves and has strong feelings or affection for the thing or person they worship. They set their affection on that thing or person, they express feelings for it, they reverence it, and they esteem it. Based on this description of what the worshipper does, it may be difficult for some to see how a follower of Christ could possibly displace worship of or love for God with worship of or love for church. Because church is good and is where we worship the Lord, some may have difficulty seeing the wrong in placing our affection on church, but keep reading, I will clarify this later.

I see four groups of worshippers in the church:

1. Relationals — those who are involved with church ministries and have a balanced life, including a dynamic and thriving personal relationship with the Lord that is marked by a disciplined and delightful prayer, Word study, and worship life.

2. Church Lifers — those who are deeply involved in church life or church ministries that mainly define their faith-walk.

3. Supplanters — those who replace personal and spiritual enrichment activities such as a disciplined prayer, Word study, and worship life with weekly church services.

4. Minimals — those who attend church intermittently, are marginally involved with church ministries, and do not engage in spiritually enriching activities outside of church.

The characteristics of these four groups are not mutually exclusive. Members of a group that fit best in one specific group can share characteristics of another group or two.

The second and third chapters of the book of Revelation detail seven letters that were written by Jesus to seven early churches located in Asia Minor. The letters were communicated to the churches by the Apostle John of Patmos. The seven churches are Ephesus, Smyrna, Pergamum, Thyatira, Sardis, Philadelphia, and Laodicea. Of the seven churches, five — Ephesus, Pergamum, Thyatira, Sardis, and Laodicea — received condemnation from Jesus and two did not — Smyrna and Philadelphia. These letters were written to seven early churches, but they are just as much for the churches of today and they are addressed to the church at the corporate level as well as to individual believers.

Based on the condemnation that Jesus gave to the churches, I align each group — Relationals, Church Lifers, Supplanters, and Minimals — with one or two of the 7 churches. This does not mean a group is solely limited to my interpretation of the condemnation. There is flexibility, as it depends on the angle from which one looks at the condemnation and the description given for each group of believers.

The religious community, especially larger churches, has expanded its means of sharing the gospel and interacting with believers over the years. For many years, churches have used various communication methods to reach their audiences, such as radio, television, and online media, but they were doing so while still having the option to meet in person. In fact, in-person gatherings were the primary means of sharing the gospel during those times. But the church leaders of today, due to the COVID-19 lockdown, while still being able to address their audience through various means were restricted for the very first time from having in-person gatherings. This was new for all church leaders.

Like the church leaders, this drastic limitation affected the church members, and as expected, it has had a different effect on different groups of individuals in the church. I believe the effect it has had depends on the relationship the individual had with God before the ban on corporate worship was enforced.

The cessation of corporate worship due to the COVID-19 lockdown was the litmus test for Christians today. The test is: have we chosen church over God? Have we chosen religion over a relationship with the lover of our souls? In reference to our relationship with the Lord, COVID-19 separated the girls from the women and the boys from the men. COVID-19 exposed the weaknesses in our spiritual buildings, buildings that appeared to be strong because they had not faced a test of this sort.

So, how did the restriction affect the four groups of people in the church and why?

Relationals

Relationals maintain a healthy balance between church and God. They embrace the importance of being connected with a local church, the assembling of the saints together for worship, and the importance of serving in ministry, but they are very much aware that an intimate personal relationship with God is even more important than anything church offers or requires. These individuals are more focused on establishing and maintaining an intimate relationship with God than on the dynamics of church life and its operations.

The church of Philadelphia was commended by Jesus because the brethren were strong in evangelism and were faithful. They served in ministry, shared the message of Jesus, and remained true to the Word of God. These brethren had a healthy balance between ministry work and relationship with God. Their ministry was effective because they were connected to the source through a covenant relationship.

Jesus commended the Philadelphia church for keeping the Word of the Lord. In John 14:15 (KJV) Jesus said, *"If you love Me, keep My commandments."* And the commendation in Revelation 3:10 confirms that His view of obedience to His Word has not changed.

> *Because you have obeyed my command to perse-vere, I will protect you from the great time of test-ing that will come upon the whole world to test those who belong to this world.* — Revelation 3:10, NLT

Obedience to the Word of God can only come from our love for God, which is foundational to an in-timate relationship with Him. The Philadelphia church was recognizable by the godly fruit which the congregation and the brethren bore. We cannot bear godly fruit (the fruit of the Spirit) if we are not con-nected to the Vine, which is Jesus Christ.

> *Remain in me, and I will remain in you. For a branch cannot produce fruit if it is severed from the vine, and you cannot be fruitful unless you remain in me.* – John 15:4, NLT

This connection to the Vine is an intimate rela-tionship with Christ our Lord, and it is essential to be-ing spiritually fruitful. We cannot be connected to the

Vine or in an intimate relationship with God if we don't love Him, so ultimately, the church of Philadelphia was commended by Jesus for the love relationship they had with Him.

Relationals today are like the brethren of the church of Philadelphia. They walk this faith-walk out of pure longing and love for the Father, and out of that love comes the godly fruit God expects us to bear. We are to be judged by the fruit we bear, and though we are saved by faith and not works, evidence that we are saved are the works we do and the fruit we bear. As James 2:18 (NLT) says:

> Now someone may argue, "Some people have faith; others have good deeds." But I say, "How can you show me your faith if you don't have good deeds? I will show you my faith by my good deeds.

Relationals know that a fulfilling intimate love relationship with God is personal and requires deliberate and constant attention. They know that to develop this sort of relationship with God, they must do the work — interact with and pursue Him primarily on a one-on-one and private basis, not in corporate worship. They also know that there is a place for them to work in ministry to build the Kingdom of God here on earth and so they occupy their place of service. They know that their gifts and callings are to do the work of the ministry, to edify the body of Christ, and to equip the saints (Ephesians 4:12), so they stay connected to a local assembly to be fed spiritually and to feed others spiritually.

While Relationals have intimacy with God which is marked by conversations with Him through reading the Bible (His main way of communicating with those who love Him) and prayer (a means of seeking the Lord, asking of the Lord, and knocking on heaven's door) — the main elements in their faith-walk — they also value time spent with fellow believers. They know that spending time with other believers is reciprocally beneficial and are aware that, according to Proverbs 27:17 (KJV), "*Iron sharpeneth iron; so a man sharpeneth the countenance of his friend.*"

Relationals benefit from fellowshipping with other believers as other believers show them a picture of God they might not have seen before. Other believers can teach Relationals a tremendous amount about Christ, show them His love; read and study the Bible (His Word) with them, encourage them, and pray for them. Relationals fellowship with other believers for these reasons to enrich their relationship with the Lord and to do the same for other believers.

Because Relationals have a personal, dynamic, and enduring relationship with the Lord outside of the four walls of the church building, when the doors of the church closed and they could no longer engage in corporate worship, they already had the discipline and had already cultivated a delight in spending individual and private time in prayer, in the Word, and in worship. For these individuals, a negative impact of the COVID-19 shutdown on their spiritual wellbeing would be minimal to none, and many would see the extra time as an advantage.

A negative impact of the COVID-19 shutdown would be minimal to none on Relationals because not just the ban on corporate worship but also the shut-down of society in general gave them time they did not have before to further cultivate their relationship with the Lord. It is human nature to spend energy, time, and resources where our interests lie. Based on the type of relationship Relationals have with the Lord, their interest is obviously deep intimacy with Him. So, nat-urally, they would use the extra time to further develop their interest, which is intimacy with the Lord.

Because Relationals already have an appetite for God and are already in pursuit of Him, they will most likely draw even nearer to God during this time. They will see this as an opportunity to spend more time in personal spiritual development activities.

Church Lifers

Research shows that online attendance increased in the early phase of the COVID-19 lockdown, but within a month, churches began to experience a decline of about ten percent. During the second week of Barna's weekly pastor survey (March 24-30, 2020) nearly half (45 percent) of pastors said online participation was higher than in-person service attendance. One in 3 (33 percent) said it was less and only 6 percent said it was about the same. One in 3 practicing Christians had stopped attending church during the COVID-19 pandemic, and this data points at the very early phase of the pandemic.

Data results show a steady decline in church attendance as the pandemic persisted. A month later, April 21-27, 2020, this trend started declining. About 1 in 3 church leaders said attendance was higher (35 percent), 29 percent said it was about the same, and 32 percent said it was less than normal.

A deep immersion in church activities could be mistaken for a close connection to God and one may think those who are deeply immersed in church, like the Church Lifers, would not be among those whose church attendance declined during the shutdown. However, absorption in church or ministry activities do not equate to loving God or having intimacy with Him. It is possible to work for God but not with Him, and sadly, many in Christendom are doing just that. The optimal is to work in partnership with Him, to have Him work through us, not for Him.

Sometimes, Church Lifers use ministry as a kind of badge of honor. They address needs like Jesus did, so they feel justified and honored. They can create or readily enlist themselves for a program that solve problems and meets needs in their church or community, all under the umbrella of ministry. Church Lifers often have a plan to change circumstances so that problems will be addressed, and they will fix them, all in the name of ministry.

Their success depends largely on how hard they work, how involved they are with church activities, what expertise they bring to the ministry, what information they offer, how good their ministry concepts are, and so forth. They hope that God will bless their efforts and that they will be successful in ministry because the highlight of their faith-walk is ministry, not relationship.

Their concept of success in ministry is not usually in line with what Jesus would consider successful. Often, success revolves around them, not God. So, when they are about to carry out ministry or implement a program, they will probably ask God's blessing on it and might pray afterward in thanksgiving, but none of this is about connection with God or working with God. The focus is on them. Their work is to meet their needs, which are to work the ministry and be successful while doing it. Though Church Lifers may not be cognizant of their behavior and more so their motive, this is their mindset. To them, their labor is a close walk with the Lord because they are doing His work.

Church Lifers are like the brethren in the church of Thyatira or Sardis. Both churches were at opposite ends of the spectrum. Thyatira was high on ministry work and low on spirituality and Sardis was low on ministry work but high on spirituality. Thyatira was known for executing well-organized and seemingly effective ministry activities and church programs. They were immersed in the hustle and bustle of church life but had a weak connection to the Vine.

The church of Thyatira did the mission trips, had the soup kitchens, and ran summer camps for the underprivileged. They even built homes for the poor and elderly. They created businesses in the community and trained and hired the disenfranchised. They did it all, but they worked for the Lord, not with Him because they were out of relationship with Him.

Perhaps their works or ministries were carried out because they simply wanted to help the community. Or the motive could be purely because helping others can be personally rewarding, but none of this is to the glory of God. Furthermore, the church of Thyatira tolerated false teachings from the false prophetess called Jezebel. Therefore, their Word-life was weak. This is the state of Church Lifers.

Sardis was the opposite of Thyatira. Of the five churches that got a rebuke from Jesus, this church got one of the harshest rebukes. Jesus said, "*I know all the things you do, and that you have a reputation for being alive – but you are dead*" (Revelation 3:1b, NLT). Although Church lifers worked the ministry for the wrong reasons, they will say, "*Lord! Lord! We prophesied in your name and cast out demons in your name and performed many miracles in your name*" (Matthew 7:23, NLT). But this is the response they will get, "*I never knew you. Get away from me, you who break God's laws*" (Matthew 7:23, NLT). No one wants to be told they are ineffective (dead) when they thought they were making a difference (alive). This is an indisputably searing rebuke from Jesus. The brethren of Sardis thought well of themselves and were perceived by others as alive but in the eyes of Jesus, they were dead.

They thought they were spiritually alive, and others thought the same because they held good church services. They prophesied and performed miracles all in the name of the Lord. They hosted large conferences. They brought in the most popular speakers for their conferences and the top of the chart gospel artists for their large concerts. They held prayer meetings for hours while people just outside the church doors were dying. They were wedded to their church programs and schedules. The thought of replacing a morning or afternoon service with street outreach would be nearly absurd. Their thought is they must be in the house of the Lord.

Members of the church were happy and blessed when they came to the church of Sardis. The church had the perfect sound system, awesome worship leaders, powerful preachers and teachers, and was growing in number but not in true disciples of Christ. They had television and radio broadcasts, wrote and published books and "how to" manuals, but the community of unbelievers did not know them. In fact, if the church was to shut down at any time, people in the community would not miss it. Everything they did took place inside the four walls of the church building. These are Church Lifers.

Jesus says to the church, "*I have not found thy works perfect before God*" (Revelation 3:2b, KJV). The general meaning of "works that are not complete" is simply: they don't meet the standard of Christ; they don't measure up. There is something missing from their works, and it is a crucial element.

This made their works imperfect or incomplete. The word complete means, "fulfilled." That tells us that the works of this church in Sardis were not fulfilling God's purpose for them, and we know that God's purpose for any work of the church is that it would glorify Him, nothing less. Sardis had ministries that were man-centered, not God-centered.

The ministry of this church was not done to show the supremacy of Christ. They were not to display the ultimate worth of Jesus or to demonstrate His character. Because they were so immersed in church life, the ministries might have been executed to keep the church going and to have the best church possible. It might have been done purely because having what seems to be a vibrant church can be personally rewarding, but none of that gives glory to God.

Because they were so advanced in church activities, the brethren of Sardis wrongfully thought they were alive, and their counterparts thought the same. They had a strong reputation in areas that do not indicate spiritual life, so they were spiritually dead. When Jesus told the church they were "dead," He was using the word "dead" in the same way He used it in the parable of the prodigal son when the father said in Luke 15:24 (KJV), *"For this son my son was dead, and is alive again."*

Jesus also told the church that there are a few in the church that had not soiled their garments, meaning most of them had soiled their garments. In other words, they were spiritually defiled by the sins of the world. Those with soiled garments, which is clear in Scripture that it was much of the church, were living like the world. They were busy in church ministries, but their hearts were not in the right place. Though they were active in ministry, the majority in this church were living deeply compromised lives and looked more like the world than Jesus.

Church Lifers are busy doing things in the name of Christ, but in name only. The works of Church Lifers are not motivated by a desire to honor Christ; instead, they are focused on maintaining church activities. Church is the center of their life. They are overly involved in ministries within the church, they attend most if not all services, they do very little to nothing pertaining to the Kingdom of God outside the four walls of the church, and they are wedded to customs, practices, and routines of church. Church Lifers are the ones that have a conniption if there is any variation from the usual way of doing things in the church.

Church Lifers routinely, without thought or effort, slow down or stop what they are doing weekly and find themselves in church. I worked in Alexandria, Virginia, for 20 years and lived in the same house for the same 20 years. Whenever I got in my car to go from home to work or from work to home, I did it without thinking. It was routine. It was thoughtless. I did it physically, but my mind was not in it. Church Lifers are just like that. They go to church out of routine. They do it but their heart is not where it should be. Their heart is not on the Person, Jesus Christ.

Church Lifers are the ones that will most likely neglect their duties as a wife, father, husband, or parent because of church duties. One may ask, but doesn't God come first, so isn't putting church duties before everything else the right thing to do? It is correct that God comes first, but neither church life nor church duties is God. Church is the thing and God is the Person. We must put the Person first. We must put God in the highest place in our lives.

Church Lifers are all about church — traditions, programs, ceremonies, ministries — and everything else that comes with church life. But Jesus teaches the Kingdom message, not the message of the church. The Bible is filled with parables that are all about the Kingdom of God, not church. The Kingdom of God was central to Jesus' teachings, not church.

Church Lifers are stagnant and inflexible. They are at high risk for spiritual decline and even spiritual death if they cannot engage in church life. They are less likely to acknowledge and act upon the fact that they have access to God wherever they are — no matter how unchurch-like the surroundings might be. Unlike the Relationals, Church Lifers' relationship with God is circumstantial. So, if they are not in a religious setting with all the religious props in place, they find it difficult or perhaps unable to connect with God.

The Apostle Paul's letter to the Corinthians, conveys that we are the temple of God. So, because we carry His presence, we should not need to be in a church environment or any other particular environment to connect with God.

> Don't you realize that all of you together are the temple of God and that the Spirit of God lives in you? — 1 Corinthians 3:16, NLT

In his letter to the Corinthians, Paul told Christians in that city (and us today) that God's presence wasn't only *around* them but *within* them. We are the body of Christ on earth; we are the temple of the Holy Spirit. We are living, breathing sanctuaries, so we carry God's presence with us wherever we go. Church Lifers may know this intellectually, but they fail to live it out because they are most spiritual and are most attentive to spiritual matters when in church.

The Apostle Paul's message to the Corinthian brethren (and to us) makes ludicrous the idea of needing to be in church to have proximity to God. We, the believers, are the place, the house, and the temple where God's presence dwells. We need to go inward to find God, but Church Lifers do not embrace this truth.

Let me quickly address a question that this statement might have created. I am not saying that we don't need anyone. Indeed, we need fellowship with the saints, but again, we do not need church as defined as ministry activities or a set of buildings. Fellowshipping with the saints is not church. Remember, iron sharpens iron. As John Donne said, "No man is an island entire of itself; every man is a piece of the continent." Isolation breeds death. So, we must be connected to other believers. But when church life — ceremonies, ministries, programs — become your focus, you are a Church Lifer.

Church Lifers find the church building comforting and edifying. They find inspiration and wisdom there. They can be spiritual in the church building but are less effective outside the building. But Jesus wants us to carry the gospel message with impact wherever we go. It should not be confined to or be more impactful in the house of worship. If left up to Church Lifers, the gospel would be shared only in church because everything revolves around the building and what takes place in it.

Church is important. It can help brighten the light of Christ in us, but we must not see church as our all in all. The reach of the light of Christ in us must not be limited to the four walls of the church building.

Our light must not go dim if church is removed. Unfortunately, this is the case for Church Lifers.

Supplanters

The Barna Group reported that in early part of the COVID-19 pandemic, 1 in 3 practicing Christians had stopped attending church. But why? Why do closed doors to church buildings result in any Christian disengaging from church?

As initial stay-at-home ordinances were lifting across the country, Barna surveyed thousands of Americans to see what their Sunday morning routines looked like during the COVID-19 shutdown. At that time, data showed that those who identify as Christian, agree strongly that faith was very important in their lives and reported they attended church at least monthly (prior to COVID-19). Of these respondents, results from the Barna survey show that over half (53 percent) had streamed their regular church online within the past four weeks. Another 34 percent admitted to streaming a church service other than their own, essentially "church hopping" digitally. Finally, about one-third of practicing Christians (32 percent) said they had done neither of these things. Though some of these churchgoers may have been part of the minority of congregations that were still gathering for in-person worship during those weeks, we can, for the most part, confidently interpret this group as those who dropped out of church at least for the time being.

Some respondents share that, over four weeks, they streamed both their church's online service as well as different church services, perhaps taking advantage of the variety and increase in digital options. But just over a third (35 percent) of practicing Christians say they still only attended their pre-COVID-19 church. Commitment to one's local church extended to frequency of church attendance during the shutdown but even more so when practicing Christians streamed the same church they attended before COVID-19. Those who attended online churches other than their local church were significantly more likely to attend church on a weekly basis than those who did not change churches (81 percent vs. 65 percent). This could be due to the wide range of options available online.

Survey results show that very few (14 percent) respondents made a church switch during the pandemic. The survey results show that it is more likely for a Christian to have stopped attending church altogether than to switch church during the pandemic. In fact, 32 percent of practicing Christians have done just that. The remaining 18 percent of practicing Christians were viewing worship services from multiple churches throughout the month.[15]

Supplanters are Christians that may have a church membership, but they may not attend church regularly and may not be actively involved in local church ministries. The main characteristic of Supplanters is they do very little outside of church to build their relationship with the Lord. Their personal prayer life is weak, and the only time they read their Bible is when they are in a church service. They rarely read devotionals or books to foster their spiritual development. They are not involved with cell groups, Christian book clubs, prayer groups, or any other associations that can help build them up spiritually.

Their only spiritual nourishment is what they get when they sit in the pews in church. But despite the minimal involvement of these individuals, they once loved the Lord, they got baptized, and they became a member of a local congregation.

Supplanters are like the church of Ephesus in the sense that the brethren of Ephesus had left their first love for God. Jesus highlighted their shortcoming: *"Nevertheless I have somewhat against thee, because thou hast left thy first love"* (Revelation 2:4, KJV). They no longer had the same passion for Christ as when they first believed. The love which has been left is a love which existed previously. "First" here means first in time or earliest. Some scholars posit that the love Jesus was referring to was brotherly love, not love for God, but I will refer to it here as love for God.

Supplanters show up from week to week for church services, but they have no passion for God or His people. Their misplaced affection is expressed by their apathy toward God. Publicly, they are for Christ but privately and in their minds, they have other lovers; they have other gods or idols in their lives.

They have become quite busy and preoccupied with life so that Jesus is no longer that important to them. Their relationship with the Lord has become just another part of their routine that they fit in their busy lives on weekends.

Supplanters are not passionate for God, but they still attend church. They have not left the church and gone out into the world and begun again to live a life of sin. They are still attending church, so it is not that they no longer love the Lord. They may love the Lord to some degree, but they no longer love Him the way they did when they first became Christians. So, like the church of Ephesus, they too have left their first love.

Supplanters are the opposite of the Bereans. According to Acts 17:11, the Bereans listened intently to Paul's message, and they went home and searched the Scriptures diligently to see if Paul and Silas were teaching them the truth. Whatever Supplanters get from the pulpit in their church is what they feed on. They take no further actions to learn more or verify what they hear in church.

If all the spiritual nourishment Supplanters get is from weekly congregational gatherings, they were greatly impacted in a negative way when the church doors locked because of the COVID-19 pandemic. These are the individuals who will likely not log on to virtual church services. So, the one source of spiritual nourishment dried up and so did their spirituality.

Furthermore, because Supplanters have an almost nonexistent personal prayer, Word, or worship life, they will not likely exercise any spiritual discipline to build themselves up spiritually during the shutdown. Before the shutdown, Supplanters did not have a strong desire to spend private time with the Lord in prayer, worship, or the Word, and there is a strong possibility that did not change when they were left to themselves and away from the moral support one can obtain from other believers.

Worship is not limited to the time spent in corporate worship on a weekly basis. It is a way of life, which means we spend time in private worship as well. And the more time we spend in private worship the more we love Him. This then cannot be contained when we engage in corporate worship. But because Supplanters do nothing outside of church to build themselves spiritually, even their worship in corporate settings is dry and flat, let alone what it likely became during the shutdown when they were not in the company of the saints.

According to the Apostle Paul, we all have two laws warring in our members.

But I see another law in my members, warring against the law of my mind, and bringing me into

captivity to the law of sin which is in my members.
— Romans 7:23, KJV

Whichever of these two laws we feed will be stronger and will have its way with us. Naturally, because Supplanters are not feeding their spirit, they must be feeding their flesh. So, they are the ones who most likely spent their time on inconsequential things during the shutdown. They had an appetite for the things of this world, more than the things of God. They talked about everything else other than the things of God. They enjoyed secular songs and worldly entertainment more than sacred songs. They fed themselves with the things of this world, and therefore, they built an appetite for more things of this world and not of God. The restriction on corporate worship was detrimental to these individuals because they were left to themselves to further indulge the flesh.

Minimals

The days when people attend church 50 of the 52 main worship days (Sunday or Saturday) in the year are nonexistent. Church attendance has been declining steadily for the past decade or so, well before the COVID-19 pandemic. But there is evidence that an effect of the ban on church gatherings could be a sharper decline in church attendance, and this could change the landscape of the church and how churches carry out their ministries forever.

Results from studies conducted by the Pew Research Center report that although religious beliefs and practices have been declining at a rapid pace for people of all ages, the decline has been most noticeable among the millennials. In 2019, roughly two-thirds of millennials attended worship services a few times per year or less, and 4 in 10 report that they seldom or never attended church. In 2009, about a decade ago, more than half of millennials attended worship services a few times per year or less, and only one-third rarely attended or not at all. The participants included in the Pew studies may be generally Americans — followers of Christ and not — but the audience under consideration in this discourse are those who have given their lives to the Lord.

The findings are the same for ages 18 to 29 and this sample includes churchgoers, not the general population. Barna president, David Kinnaman, in his 2011 book, *You Lost Me*, report that 59 percent of young adults with a Christian background had dropped out of church at some point during their 20s — many temporarily, but some for good. In 2019, research results for Kinnaman's book, *Faith for Exiles: Five Ways for a New Generation to Follow Jesus in Digital Babylon,* indicate that the church dropout problem persisted. In fact, the percentage of young-adult dropouts had increased from 59 to 64 percent. A whopping two-thirds of Americans between 18 and 29 years of age who grew up in church had withdrawn from church involvement as an adult after having been active as a child or teen.

We know that a leading cause for the decline in church attendance is the proliferation of online churches and social media platforms by which the gospel can be preached. Millennials are the first technological generation, so naturally, with the ubiquity of these options, many will not or barely step foot in a church building.

There are other reasons why millennials may stop attending church. First, many millennials never had strong ties to religion to begin with, which means they were less likely to develop habits or associations that make it easier to return to a religious community after exploring other options. Second, an increasing number of young adults are marrying outside of the faith; they are more likely to have a spouse who is not religious, which may help reinforce their secular worldview. Finally, changing views about the relationship between morality and religion also appear to have convinced many young parents that religious institutions are simply irrelevant or unnecessary for their children.[16]

The discussion so far is about individuals who stopped attending church altogether or have stopped church attendance and have switched to online platforms but let us now look more closely at the Minimals, those who were attending church before COVID-19 but were barely involved. How did the ban on church gatherings affect them? If millennials or anyone of any age group were barely attending church prior to COVID-19, the social move to solely attend church services virtually will likely result in a cessation of church attendance for them.

Church attendance hinges heavily on church or ministry engagement. In fact, engagement is far more important than attendance. Church attendance will very likely wane if someone merely attends a church week after week but does not serve in any capacity or attend any cell group or community group meetings in the church.

There could be any number of reasons why a Christian would be barely involved in a local church. Some will tell you they don't see the relevance of church or the direct benefit of being in church. This lack of relevance could be simply because the church is dispensing information and executing ministries that are not meaningful or practical to the people. Also, it could be due to the individual's lack of connection with the things of God. The church could be doing all the right things, but if the people's hearts are not ready to receive and engage what the church ministries are dispensing, the people will view the ministry as irrelevant. It is less likely these people will see themselves as the ones who, because of their disengagement with God, cannot receive the treasures of the ministry.

As humans, we make time for things we value most. Minimals will least likely adjust their schedule to make room for a church event because church is not a priority for them. With extra time given by the lockdown and because the things of God are not valued enough, Minimals will not spend their time doing things to build their or others' spirituality.

Minimals could be any age group, but the majority may be millennials. Millennials may be leading the charge on the shift away from religion, but they did not initiate it. Their parents are at least partly responsible for a widening generational gap in religious identity and beliefs. Young adults were more likely than previous generations to be raised without any connection to organized religion. According to the American Enterprise Institute survey, compared with only 5 percent of Baby Boomers, 17 percent of millennials said they were not raised in a specific religion. And compared with about half (49 percent) of Baby Boomers, fewer than 1 in 3 (32 percent) millennials say they attended weekly religious services with their family when they were young. This sets the foundation for millennials to be Minimals.

Minimals are like the church of Laodicea. Jesus told this church, "*I know your works: you are neither cold nor hot. Would that you were either cold or hot! So, because you are lukewarm, and neither hot nor cold, I will spit you out of my mouth*" (Revelation 3:15–16, NIV). Lukewarmness refers to Christians who are indifferent or apathetic because they are self-satisfied or complacent.

Lukewarm Christians believe they are in good standing with God, but this is not the case.

God wished the Laodiceans were hot or cold but that is not because He wants His people to have cold hearts toward Him. He is saying they are lukewarm because they have lost their dependence on Him.

Verse 17 says, "*You say, 'I am rich; I have acquired wealth and do not need a thing.' But you do not realize that you are wretched, pitiful, poor, blind and naked.*" Lukewarm could mean a person who is mildly passionate about God, but that is not what God was saying. God was saying that the lukewarmness was their arrogance, the belief they have no need of Christ's righteousness because they have enough of their own. This is exactly the mindset of those who see it fit to disengage with the church. The lukewarm (Minimals) are spiritually sick and near death.

The Apostle Paul says to the Roman believers in Roman 12:11 (NIV), "*Never be lacking in zeal, but keep your spiritual fervor, serving the Lord.*" The meaning of *spiritual fervor* is to be spiritually hot, meaning on fire for God. Something or someone that is on fire will radiate; they will glow, especially in the dark. God wants us to be light in this dark world. He wants us to be on fire and burn with passion for Him.

A person who is hardly engaged in a local congregation and does not participate in spiritually enriching activities outside of church will not be fervent for God. This describes the Minimals. Without this connection to God, a complete shut down from the only source they were getting sporadic spiritual feeding likely resulted in further spiritual decline.

The Unanswered Questions

There are a few very important questions that I must introduce before moving on. First, what is more important to today's believers, to which one are we wedded, church or God? What or who are we really worshipping, the Person or the thing? What is that thing we are worshipping? Why would not being able to go inside a building for church services result in any believer stop attending church when the doors reopened? Why would any believer decline spiritually while the doors of the church were closed due to a pandemic? Why is it that in the aftermath of the ban on corporate worship due to COVID-19 many pastors, especially of small churches, claim they will have to rebuild because their membership has gone down? Why are many saying there are members of their church that have become blatantly non-responsive or that they are nowhere to be found? These people have fallen off the church wagon. Why has this happened? Why is it that after the release to return to congregational worship, gospel stations are now running advertisements to encourage people to return to church? Why is that necessary?

The discussion thus far has been centered around the impact of COVID-19, but the response of believers to the shutdown on corporate worship is not due to the ban on worship; it is deeper than that. The response due to the COVID-19 lockdown is merely a symptom of the real problem. Each person's response reflects who they are wedded to, who they truly worship, and the place upon which they have set their affection.

Going forward, I will take a general stance as I continue to discuss our relationship with God and what God wants in a relationship with His people.

The Early Churches and Today's Church at a Glance

Early Church	Commonality Between the Early Church and Today's Church	Today's Church
Ephesus	Left their first love.	Supplanters
Thyatira	Lots of works / ministry activities. Lack spiritual power.	Church Lifers
Sardis	Have spiritual power but no works, no ministry activities.	Church Lifers
Philadelphia	Strong in and have good balance between works, ministry activities, and spiritual power. Vital faith relationship with God.	Relationals
Laodicea	Lukewarm. Jesus said He will spew/vomit the lukewarm out of His mouth.	Minimals

Church Lifers can be found at either end of the spectrum — lots of ministry activities but no spiritual power or very embedded in church (spiritual) but no ministry activities.

4

FAMILIARITY BREEDS CONTEMPT

In 2016, I was on my way to vacation in Utah. I was scheduled to speak at a church in New York shortly after returning from vacation. I boarded the plane, settled in my seat, and closed my eyes. Not long after the plane lifted, I heard a still small voice inside me say, "Remind my people of who I am." I knew immediately what the Lord wanted me to convey to the beloved brethren to whom I would soon be ministering.

The title of the sermon I preached was "God Is," but I could have just as well titled the sermon "Familiarity Breeds Contempt." God wanted me to tell His people who He is because they did not *know* Him. I was to *remind* them because they had once known Him, but they had forgotten who He is. They had become familiar with Him.

The expression "familiarity breeds contempt" was first used in English in the 1300s by Geoffrey Chaucer in his work, *Tale of Melibee*. It simply means that the more we know someone or the longer we are around someone, the more we take them for granted, producing carelessness and lack of respect. The proverb also means that the better we know people, the more likely we are to find fault with them (The New Dictionary of Cultural Literacy) or the more we know something or someone, the more we start to find faults and dislike things about it or them (UsingEnglish.com).

A pivotal question that I ask in this book is: church or God? This question could be asked another way: religion or relationship? or The Person or the thing? The Person being God, and the thing being anything but God. For many believers, the thing is not anything bad, sinful, or evil. In fact, for these believers, the thing is good. The thing is church or anything related to church, such as ministry activities like soup kitchens to feed the hungry, mission trips, visits to the sick, religious ceremonies such as baptisms, Lord's Supper or Communion, and church events like conferences, retreats, prayer meetings, and weekly worship services.

The question — Church or God? — is asking if we have come to love church and its associated activities more than we love the God that the true church, His people, are called to worship. Our affection will shift from the Person (God) to the thing (church) when we lose our awe for Him, when we become familiar with Him. This is what happens when we become accustomed to Him. Church then becomes a part of our lives. It becomes something we routinely do, and usually, in becoming familiar with God, we also become familiar with His house. We treat attending church mindlessly, and we approach His house and conduct ourselves in His house irreverently.

This should not be the case but many who have been walking with the Lord for a while have become familiar with Him. Definitions for "familiarity" from Oxford Languages are "close acquaintance with or knowledge of something, the quality of being well known, recognizability based on long or close association, relaxed friendliness, or intimacy between people."

Familiarity with God is expressed in many ways by believers. But I believe two of the most expressive manifestations of such a mindset toward God are a lack of awe of Him and a lack of desire to know Him deeply or more deeply.

The absence of awe of God is a very dangerous place to be. When we no longer have a sense of wonder about Him, we lower our expectations of Him, and we don't look for the supernatural from Him. Therefore, we worship and pray because that's what Christians do, but we have no expectation of His presence. Said differently, we pray religiously but don't expect God to answer.

This gives Him no room to work because He works according to our expectations...no expectation of Him means no movement from Him. He promises in Ephesians 3:20 that He will exceed what we ask or think, but that depends on the power that works in us. That power is the expectation, the faith that looks for God to do something.

We should want to know the Lord deeply and have an intimate relationship with Him. This must be a life-long pursuit of all devoted followers of Christ. In fact, the more we come to know Him the more we will find we need to seek Him. This kind and gracious God of ours is inexhaustible. He is past finding out. He is unascertainable, and it is an absolute joy to seek Him endlessly. The encounters with Him are life-changing and cannot be experienced any other way. Therefore, a hunger and thirst for the God of our salvation ought to be fundamental to all believers.

We should never become familiar with God, and it is a hunger for Him that will safeguard us from becoming familiar with Him. He is too great, multifaceted, unfathomable, supreme, incomprehensible, and the list can go on, for any created being to become familiar with Him. This is the grave danger that many of today's believers have fallen into. Many of us have been serving the Lord for so long that He has now become just another aspect of our lives.

It is no different from a love relationship. New lovers seek to please each other, they cannot stop staring at each other, they are eager to learn about each other, they look forward to spending time together, they don't want to stop talking to each other, and they don't want to go anywhere without each other. For a period of time, they are both in a discovery mode of each other. They are love-struck and in admiration of each other. But with time — much sooner for some than others —they eventually become familiar with one another. With God, we should be in discovery mode always. And the beauty here is, He rewards those who seek Hm diligently (Hebrews 11:6). A few other scriptures that direct us to seek God diligently are:

Seek the LORD and his strength, seek his face continually. – 1 Chronicles 16:11, KJV

The LORD is good unto them that wait for him, to the soul that seeketh him. — Lamentations 3:25, KJV

But seek ye first the kingdom of God, and his righteousness; and all these things shall be added unto you. — Matthew 6:33, KJV

No one seeks out anything or anyone with which they are already familiar. We seek out what we need to know and what we want to experience more of. Familiarity kills our hunger for the Lord.

Inevitably, a longtime church going Christian will become familiar with church dynamics and operations, but church life should never become that other thing we do. Despite how long we are doing these things, when serving in ministry or when going into the house of the Lord, we should realize the utmost importance of what we are doing, whey we are doing it, and for whom we are doing it. If we become familiar with church, we are in grave danger of becoming familiar with God or vice versa. I believe people will more often become familiar with God (the Person) before they become familiar with church (the thing). Our relationship with God is vital to our faith-walk. So, if our relationship with God is poor, everything else in our walk with the Lord will be affected.

Familiarity with the House of God

We know we are familiar with church when we stop looking forward to or anticipate going to church. We are familiar with church when it becomes just another weekly activity. Another sign of familiarity with church is when we have no expectation when we go to church. We know the routine or program and we expect nothing more and nothing less than the activities on the weekly program. Furthermore, we are quite content when we get nothing when we go to church or when the weekly church services are scripted, predictable, and programmed. We are familiar with church when we have no desire for more.

The building in which worship services take place is called the church, the house of the Lord, the house of God, or the sanctuary. Webster's dictionary also offers a religious definition: "a house consecrated to the worship of God; a place where divine service is performed." The definition goes on to refer to the Old Testament, where the word sanctuary indicates "the most sacred part of the tabernacle, called the holy of holies, in which the ark of the covenant was kept, and into which no person was allowed to enter except the High Priest, and that only once a year to intercede for the people." This is a set apart, a holy place where God meets with His people.

When Jesus offered His life on Calvary as the perfect sacrifice for the sins of mankind, He gave us access into that holy place which previously had been forbidden to the common man. We read in Hebrews 9:12 that Christ, by the shedding of His own blood, entered once and for all into the holy place, and by so doing, obtained eternal redemption for us. We no longer need a middleman. We no longer need a high priest to go into the holy place on our behalf. Now we — ordinary men and women — can enter the sanctuary and speak with God ourselves. The holy place where the priests went once yearly was a sacred place and so is our houses of worship, our church buildings today. God has high regard for this place.

> [15] Now my eyes will be open and my ears attentive to the prayers offered in this place. [16] I have chosen and consecrated this temple so that my Name may be there forever. My eyes and my heart will always be there. – 2 Chronicles 7:15-16, NIV

When God declared that He would be attentive to prayers made in "this place," He was referring to any physical location that is dedicated to host His people for worship. That is anywhere the people of God gather to worship Him. People can gather to worship and pray in the mountains, by a river, in the woods, or in private homes, and God will meet them there. While the ad hoc locations — such as a person's living room — can be used for multiple purposes, it must also be recognized and treated like a place of worship when the space is used for this reason. This *place* of worship, be it an ad hoc site or a dedicated sanctuary, is a place with which we must not become familiar.

A house of worship is called a sanctuary because it provides a safe place, a place of refuge where we can be fed spiritually and where our faith can be built up. Having access to this sacred place is a privilege, and we must treat it with reverence. Though we enter this place quite frequently, we must not become familiar with it. If we do, we will lose the honor and respect it deserves, and we will lose honor and respect for the Person of the place.

We know we are familiar with church when we lose reverence for the place of worship, the house of God. A loss of reverence for the house of God can be shown in many ways. If we honor and revere God, we will honor and revere His house. This is why people who are familiar with the house of God — people who do not reverence the house of God — are also familiar with God, meaning they do not reverence God. It is impossible to separate the two.

I grew up in an era when we were taught to reverence God's house. We couldn't run in church. We couldn't slouch down in the bench, no matter how long the services were. We couldn't chew gum in church, let alone eat in church. Today, I am amazed at how we — congregants and church leaders alike — treat God's house. The sanctuary is not a dining room, a meeting hall, or a place for socialization, a place women go to show off their bodies, a place to seek a spouse, or a marketplace, but today, it is often treated as such.

Jesus, in anger, overturned the tables of the money changers and cast out those who were buying and selling in the temple because they were dishonoring His house. He declared that His house is a house of prayer, but they had made it a den of thieves (Matthew 21:13). When we become familiar with His house, we do all manner of things in it. For example, people have conversations about frivolous things that have no relevance to why they are there.

The overriding purpose for going to God's house is to praise and worship Him. This is where God's glory dwells. The sound that comes from these buildings should be the sound of praise, worship, and prayer. God said that His ears would be attentive *"to the prayer that is made in this place"* (2 Chronicles 7:15) not the conversations and chatter that go on in there.

Today, the irreverence in God's house is so pervasive that it is seen while services are in progress. You find people talking, scrolling through their phone, texting, and walking in and out of the sanctuary while the Word of God is being read, taught, or preached. People also seem to see nothing wrong with walking in and out of the sanctuary and having their own conversation while prayer is being offered and during altar calls while precious souls are seeking something from the Lord.

Other ways we know we are familiar with or have lost reverence for God's house is when we are no longer joyful in the house of worship. We no longer enjoy the presence of the Lord. This is when church becomes mundane. We arrive late and leave early. We make no adjustments to our schedule to accommodate additional church activities, and weekly church services no longer take precedence on our schedule.

These important religious gatherings can easily be replaced with the slightest demand on our time. In fact, we go to church because we have been doing it for years, but that is as much as it means. We may go because if we don't go, the pastor or some members of the church will ask about us not being there. Therefore, we go because others expect us to be there. We no longer go because we look forward to meeting the God we love and serve. We no longer go because we have a sacrifice to offer our God.

We the body of Christ must not take a casual approach to our houses of worship as if they are commonplace. If we were expecting to meet with a significant figure such as the U.S. President, or a prime minister of a country, or the queen of England, we would dress for the occasion and approach the meeting with the respect due to the dignitary. When we go to our houses of worship, we are going there to meet with the All-mighty God! He is far more worthy of honor and reverence than any individual on this earth, and we must treat His house accordingly.

Most churches have a foyer and multiple rooms in the building — e.g., offices, classrooms, fellowship hall, kitchen, coat rooms. But the part of the building where the saints gather to worship is different from any other room. This is a special place. It is different. It is the sanctuary, the place set aside for worship. It is where we meet with God.

The sanctuary is like the holy of holies, which was the innermost chamber in the tabernacle. This was a sacred place where only one person, the high priest, could enter and this was done only one day out of the entire year. Jesus, through His death, gave us full access to this innermost place. Through His love and power, He ripped the thick, embroidered veil that separated the holy of holies from another room called the holy place. Consequently, we no longer need a priest to go in on our behalf. We are welcomed in this innermost place to fellowship with our God ourselves.

The holy of holies was one room in the tabernacle but there were other rooms. The other rooms were a part of the tabernacle, but they were not the holy of holies. Similarly, the other rooms in our contemporary church buildings are a part of the building but they are not the set-aside place where we meet with God. However, these rooms should be treated as a part of the tabernacle or the church building. The entire building is God's house.

Psalm 100:4 (KJV) says, "*Enter into his gates with thanksgiving, and into his courts with praise: be thankful unto him, and bless his name.*" We could consider the church parking lot up to the doorway of the sanctuary and any room but the sanctuary as "*His gates*" and the sanctuary as "*His courts.*" Therefore, our minds should be set on God — filled with thanksgiving and praise — no matter where in the building we are. That means, the coat room, the restrooms, the fellowship hall, the hallways, anywhere that is not the sanctuary should still be treated with reverence. This is so because as long as we are in the building, we must maintain the reason for being there and we must act like we know whose house we are in.

We see evidence of the superiority of "this place" when Moses approached the burning bush. God called to him, saying, "'*Do not come any closer,*' God said. '*Take off your sandals, for the place where you are standing is holy ground*'" (Exodus 3:5, NIV). The ground was not holy because of its location or because the bush that burned was not consumed. It was holy because God was there!

The meaning of *"place"* in *"the place where you are standing"* is the same root word used in 2 Chronicles 7:15-16 (NIV), which says, *"Now my eyes will be open and my ears attentive to the prayers offered in* <u>*this place*</u>. *I have chosen and consecrated this temple so that my Name may be there forever. My eyes and my heart will always be there"* (emphasis added). What is common between the burning bush and the house of the Lord in Solomon's day was that God was there. So, when we gather in *"this place"* in our day, we must be conscious of the fact that God is there. And what kind of behavior is appropriate for His presence?

Scripture tells us that the queen of Sheba, after hearing *"of the fame of Solomon concerning the name of the Lord"* (1 Kings 10:1, KJV), came to question Solomon to see if what she heard was true. She learned more about Solomon than she expected because she recognized his love for the Lord just by the way he went up into the house of God (verse 5). So that means there is a way we can enter the house of God that reflects our reverence for God's house. This might be why in times past the first thing people did when they entered a house of worship was to kneel and pray. Now we enter God's house, plop ourselves down in our seats and that's it. For some, the first thing they do is start chattering with their neighbor. We no longer pray first when we enter God's house.

Psalm 95:6 speaks of reverencing God in a different way. We read, "*O come, let us worship and bow down: let us kneel before the Lord our maker.*" Kneeling before the Lord is an expression of our reverence of Him. We come to the house of God to honor Him, and we should indicate that by kneeling before Him in prayer and worship. This is a lost virtue because we now enter our places of worship carelessly as if we are entering any place else.

Actions that show we honor and respect the house of God would be that of joy, worship, a prayerful attitude, and praise offerings, including sacrificial praise. These are praises that are not offered out of obligation or because the worship leader is "forcing" the congregation to praise God. No, they are praises that we offer to God even when we don't feel like praising Him or when things are not going as desired.

We must show our reverence for the Lord by the way we come into His house and by the way we act when we are in His house. It is entirely scriptural to reverence the house of God. Leviticus 19:30 (KJV) says, "*Ye shall keep my sabbaths, and <u>reverence my sanctuary</u>; I am the Lord*" (emphasis added).

Familiarity with God

The people that are at highest risk of breeding contempt toward God are those who have been walking with the Lord for a while. And there could be a secondary impact of familiarity on newer Christians through learned behavior. One cannot become familiar with something or a person unless they have been in contact with or exposed to the person or thing for a prolonged period. So, while not exclusive to them, it is the long-time Christians that are most at risk of becoming familiar with God.

It is the long-time Christians that can predict the scripture the preacher is going to quote. They can rattle off scriptures because they have heard them so many times throughout the years. But since the amazement of God has waned, the words are void of faith and are detached from the heart. God wants us to be continuously amazed by who He is, not by what He can do. He wants us to have an unsatiable desire to know and experience Him — His personality, His person, His heart — not His capabilities. I purposely use the word unsatiable here instead of insatiable because insatiable would mean that it is nearly impossible to satisfy, whereas unsatiable means that it is absolutely impossible to satisfy. Our Heavenly Father wants us to have such a hunger for Him that it is impossible to satisfy that hunger, which means we would always be pursuing Him for more.

Like a lack of reverence for the house of God, familiarity with God results in a lack of reverence for Him. Today, virtues like reverence and respect appear to be things of the past. Older people are grieved by the nonchalant lack of respect for the elderly, for those in authority, and for the law of the land, and these behaviors are not just among unbelievers, but are also very present among believers.

This level of contempt among older people is miniscule to the contempt for God being discussed here. We must also note that older people can lack reverence for God even though they are disturbed by the lack of respect frequently displayed today. Familiarity with God and the resulting contempt spans across all ages.

All Christians know that Jesus loves us. We know that He died for us on the cross of Calvary and that out of His unconditional everlasting love, He willingly left heaven and endured the curse of sin on our behalf. We all know the gospel very well, but have we become callous to it? Has the good news of the gospel become news as usual? Has it become old news? Is the novelty and amazement of it gone? We know we have lost our sense of awe, gratitude, and praise for the sacrifice of the Son of God when we are no longer moved by the gospel, when we lose the wonder and awe over God's incredible grace and gift to us.

Several things can point to our familiarity with God, but a significant one is a lack of expectation from God. God told me to remind His people who He is because they had forgotten who He is. Note, God did not say, "Remind my people of what I can do." No, He said, "Remind them of who I am." We must pursue the Giver, not the gifts. Familiarity with God will take our eyes off Him and as a result expect nothing extraordinary or supernatural from Him. God has lost His superiority in the lives of those who have become familiar with Him. They have no supernatural expectation from the supernatural God, so they just engage in church life — superficially or totally immersed — but expecting nothing from God.

Jesus experienced contempt due to familiarity when He went to His hometown Nazareth. This is the way people in Jesus' day felt about Him and prophets in their own towns because they knew them *before* they started prophesying and convicting them of their ungodly ways. Just before going to Nazareth, Jesus was in Galilee:

> [14] *Jesus returned to Galilee in the power of the Spirit, and news about him spread through the whole countryside.* [15] *He was teaching in their synagogues, and everyone praised him."* — Luke 4:14-15, NIV

Clearly, we see that Jesus was highly effective while ministering in Galilee. "*Everyone praised him*" because He was making a difference. He operated in "*the power of the Spirit*" while in Galilee, so people were being healed and delivered. The Galileans received Him because they knew Him. They were witnesses to what He did in Jerusalem at the feast because they were there. They had a personal experience with Him.

But then, when He was in Cana of Galilee where He turned the water into wine, there was a certain royal official, whose son was sick at Capernaum. He wanted Jesus to come to his house and heal his dying son. Jesus' response to him was this: *"Unless you people see signs and wonders...you will never believe"* (John 4:48, NIV).

While we do come to know our God by what He can do, there is a deeper level of knowing Him. I believe Jesus answered the royal official who requested prayer for his dying son as sharply as He did because this man demonstrated limited knowing of Him, and he was asking only because he had seen what Jesus had done at the wedding. He also thought Jesus had to be present with the child to heal him.

Jesus wants us to know Him beyond what He can do for us. He wants us to *know* His character and His heart. Jesus' comment was due to His frustration with people's hardness of heart who simply could not believe His teachings about living by faith in the will and essence of God without seeing the great works or miracles that He could do. But even after seeing His great works, their belief in Jesus was limited. They had not encountered the heart of Jesus. They did not *know* Him. We must believe in the God He is and His nature, not what He can do.

Things were worse in Nazareth because that was the town in which He was brought up. Those people knew Him as Mary and Joseph's son, but they knew nothing of His works. They had no experience with Him except that He was a carpenter's son. So, while in the synagogue, He unrolled the scroll of the prophet Isaiah and read:

> [18] *"The Spirit of the Lord is on me, because he has anointed me to proclaim good news to the poor. He has sent me to proclaim freedom for the prisoners and recovery of sight for the blind, to set the oppressed free,* [19] *to proclaim the year of the Lord's favor."* – Luke 4:18-19, NIV

He then added, *"Today this scripture is fulfilled in your hearing"* (verse 21b). The response of those in the synagogue was contempt because of their familiarity with Him, and Jesus knew this. Before they could tell Him, He told them, *"no prophet is accepted in his hometown"* (verse 24b).

After He pointed out to them how contemptuous the Israelites were to Elijah, implying they are doing the very same to Him, the people became furious:

> [29] *They got up, drove him out of the town, and took him to the brow of the hill on which the town was built, in order to throw him off the cliff.* [30] *But he walked right through the crowd and went on his way.* – Luke 4:29-30, NIV

> [5] *The contempt of the people impacted His work greatly. He could not do any miracles there, except*

lay his hands on a few sick people and heal them.
6 And he was amazed at their lack of faith. –
Mark 6:5-6, NIV

Could our familiarity with God be hindering
His mighty move in the church? Could our familiarity
with God be the cause for having Bible studies, prayer
meetings, and worship services void of the power of
God while we are oblivious of His absence and are
quite fine with our current powerless state?

Indicators of Familiarity with God

We have discussed church attendance as an indicator
of familiarity with God, but I want to reiterate that the
number one indicator of familiarity with God is a loss
of awe — the wow factor — in our God. One evidence
of this is the ease at which we can miss church services
and other opportunities to worship with other believers and hear the Word of God. God is the Word, and
the Word is Him (John 1:1), so the best way to know
God is to know His Word. Any believer who is not becoming lukewarm toward God but is seeking to know
Him at a deeper level will want to know His Word.

This positioning in God will keep individuals
faithful to the gathering of the saints and the study of
God's Word and will play a significant role in developing the discipline to engage in personal, private study
and other spiritual development activities on their
own. They will see these things as fuel that will keep

them ablaze for God and as necessary spiritual nourishment that if not received will lead to spiritual death.

Among other indicators, familiarity with God will be evidenced by prayerlessness or quick mindless routine utterances called prayer, no personal fasts, low expectations from God and from the ministry, apathy, and comfort with mediocrity and the status quo.

Prayerlessness

Regular times of fervent prayer seeking the face of God will be nonexistent in the lives of those who are familiar with Him. Or if the will to pray does exist, it is so weak that it does not move to action. Larry Lee introduced the concept I call the three Ds — Desire, Discipline, and Delight. To cultivate or maintain a desire to know God, we must progress from desire to discipline, and ultimately find delight in fellowshipping with Him corporately and privately.

Those who are familiar with God had at least a desire to pray in the past, but because they have gotten accustomed to God, they now show contempt for Him with a lack of desire to spend time talking to Him in prayer. Their walk with the Lord is now just another aspect of their lives, so that they are no longer eager to spend time with Him.

Familiarity with God comes at a high price spiritually. One cost is the failure to put God at the head of our lives. Without a disciplined prayer life, we will not make God the head of our lives. And without Him being the head of our lives, we will certainly stray. Whether we acknowledge it or not, our lives will be worthless if God does not lead us. Secondly, without a disciplined prayer life, we forfeit the abiding presence of God. What greater blessing is there than to know that we host His presence? These are treasures that we can access only if we are in covenant relationship with Him.

No Personal Fasts

Like a personal prayer life, personal fasts — fasts that are not called and organized by church leaders or any-one else and that are often not done with anyone else — require a drive to know God more deeply. Once we become familiar with God, we no longer have this hun-ger for Him. Familiarity puts Him in the same category as is everything else that is not of real importance to us, and normally we don't make personal sacrifices for an-yone or anything that is not important to us. There-fore, if God is moved from the highest place in our lives to one of familiarity, we probably will not see the need for personal fasts.

When we fast, we tell God that He is important to us. We tell Him that we want Him more than food or entertainment or anything else we're fasting from. Fasts also discipline us. When we can put aside what we love dearly — often food — for a season just to seek the Lord, we empower ourselves to better put the flesh under subjection. Fasting empowers us to put self under control. Fasting takes us to a place of power and anointing that we cannot experience otherwise.

Low Expectations from God and the Ministry

When I was a child, I had very high regard for my dad. Whatever he said was gospel. I also know that if I felt unsafe, my father could protect me. If I needed anything, he would provide it. If I had questions, he could answer them. It didn't matter if these things were true; that was my perspective of him. My view of him gave me that level of confidence in him. I had expectations of my father because he was the person I looked up to. I had high regard for him, and as long as that was the case, my expectations of him were high, probably higher than he could meet because he was a natural man, not God.

As it was with my earthly father, so and even more so should it be with our Heavenly Father, especially if we keep Him in His rightful place. God belongs in the highest place in our lives. He should be number one to us. He should be of utmost importance and amazement to us. But when we take Him down from the throne of our lives and place an idol in His place, we lose confidence in Him and therefore have lower expectations of Him.

These are the people who go to church week after week and expect nothing to happen. In fact, they are quite satisfied with some singing and a sermon, nothing more is expected. They forget that God is unpredictable, that we cannot limit Him to a program. They forget that church gatherings are meant to minister to the Lord and that when we minister to Him, He will come in the assembly of the saints and do wonders, like mending broken hearts, healing the sick, delivering them that are bound, saving the lost, and much more.

We should go to church expecting to see these things happen. But when we become accustomed to Him, He becomes just another element of our lives. So, we get up like robots weekly or as often as we do, get dressed for church, go to church expecting the usual, we get the usual, and we go back to our lives fully satisfied, content with low or no expectation that result from familiarity with God. Many of these people pray and confess that they believe in prayer. But because of familiarity, they pray with little to no expectation, and as a result, get little to no result.

I remember a few years ago, a speaker at the church I was attending at the time called for those with high blood pressure to come to the altar for prayer at the end of his sermon. After the service ended, I crossed path with a sister in the Lord who had gone to the altar in response to the call. As is customary when greeting someone, I asked how she was doing, and immediately she gave me a detailed account of the woes she was experiencing due to high blood pressure.

This is a classic example of praying without expectation. She was just prayed for, yet she was quick to announce what she was experiencing due to the condition. Clearly, she did not expect anything to happen. If she was expecting a change, despite the presence of the physical symptoms of high blood pressure, she would at least mention that she was looking to the Lord for healing. But nothing to that end was mentioned. All she focused on was the sickness. To a person with a mindset like that, prayer is clearly just something they do. Such a person has become accustomed to God and, as a result, has little to no expectation of Him. She went to the altar for prayer, but her confessions right after being prayed for did not point to or express expectation of improvement in her health.

Comfort with Mediocrity and the Status Quo

Mediocrity is average, and status quo is the normal existing situation, so the believers who are comfortable with mediocrity and the status quo are not seeking to grow in the Lord, neither are they seeking to advance the ministry. They want things to remain the same; no changes are needed.

Pastors and church leaders who are comfortable with mediocrity and the status quo are quite satisfied if all slots on the weekly church program are filled and church activities are executed as planned — nothing more and nothing less. These beloved ones are stagnant and don't know it. They do not have a desire for more of God, so they do nothing different to experience Him differently. In their eyes, all is well, and nothing needs to change. They are complacent. This sounds very much like the church in Laodicea who thought they were rich but in Jesus' eyes were poor.

Those who settle for mediocrity also do not consciously seek to grow. As followers of Christ, we must have an earnest desire to be like Christ. This is something we must pursue intentionally. We cannot simply go to church and expect to change. Our thoughts are not like Jesus' thoughts, and neither are our ways like His (Isaiah 55:8). Therefore, we must seek to obtain the information and expose ourselves to the materials, training, individuals, and experiences that will foster our transformation into Christlikeness.

If, for example, the members of an assembly, especially the leaders, are satisfied with things as is and do not seek to grow, they will be feeding on recycled spiritual food. The leaders especially should be feeding from a different place than the congregants so that they can bring fresh bread to the people. If no one is seeking more, they will plateau, impeding their growth in the Lord.

My dear brothers and sisters in Christ, we must be aware of the dangers of familiarity with God. We must guard our hearts with all diligence (Proverbs 4:23).

5

IDOLATRY IN DISGUISE

I dolatry is the act of replacing the one true God with another object of worship. We are guilty of idolatry when we worship anything or anyone other than the God of the universe.

God is clear. He does not share His glory. In fact, Exodus 34:14 says His name is Jealous and in Exodus 20:5, where He warns against idolatry, He clearly states that He is a jealous God. Jealousy precedes anger, it causes fury, it shows no mercy, and it takes revenge (Proverbs 6:34). So clearly, jealousy can be a destructive emotional response, but God is jealous in a loving way. He is jealous in a righteous way. God by nature is good so He is without sin. His jealousy is in response to the sin of idolatry, and it is a righteous and holy reaction to this presumptuous sin. God is jealous of idolatry because we belong to Him, no one else. We are married to Him, so He rightly wants our love and worship, and He hates it when we stray to worship something else.

God wants a relationship with man. He created us for that very reason. Man is His prize creation. Of everything that God created, man was the only created being who He did not speak into existence. When He wanted the waters, He said, "Let there be...," for the beasts of the fields and the fowls of the air, He said, "Let there be...." But to create man, God knelt in the earth and with His own hands carved out man in His likeness and then breathed Himself into us so that we can connect with Him and Him with us. The beasts of the fields, fowls of the air, and creatures of the sea cannot connect with God because He does not live in them. They were not created in His image. God did not breathe Himself into them. They cannot worship God and God does not seek or desire a relationship with them neither does He expect them to worship Him.

God created man to worship Him only and that is what He expects. He made us so that we may find our greatest joy in Him. He made us for His pleasure, for His glory, and for fellowship with Him. This does not mean God is lacking anything or is needy. He won't be any less of the supreme God He is if man does not worship Him. Whether man worships Him or not, He will be worshipped because He is God. In Luke 19, when the multitude was worshipping Jesus and the Pharisees wanted Him to rebuke them, He told them that if they did not worship and praise Him, the stones would cry out:

37 And when he was come nigh, even now at the descent of the mount of Olives, the whole multitude of the disciples began to rejoice and praise God with a loud voice for all the mighty works that they had seen; 38 Saying, Blessed be the King that cometh in the name of the Lord: peace in heaven, and glory in the highest. 39 And some of the Pharisees from among the multitude said unto him, Master, rebuke thy disciples. 40 And he answered and said unto them, I tell you that, if these should hold their peace, the stones would immediately cry out. – Luke 19:37-40, KJV

God is jealous for His relationship with us because He passionately loves us and does not want us to be destroyed by idolatry. His love for us was fully demonstrated in His sacrificial death for us. We also see His love and desire for relationship with man in the case of Adam. God walked with Adam and Eve in the Garden. In the cool of the day, He came looking for Adam:

8Then the man and his wife heard the sound of the Lord God as he was walking in the garden in the cool of the day, and they hid from the Lord God among the trees of the garden. 9 But the Lord God called to the man, "Where are you?" – Genesis 3:8-9, NIV

I believe it was customary for God to fellowship with Adam and Eve. That is why they hid themselves when they realized the sin they had committed. God had a close relationship with them, and He desires the same with us today. That is why He executed the plan of redemption, a plan that He had in His heart before the foundation of the world (Ephesians 1:4-5). What a blessing, a privilege, and an honor to know the high and lifted One, the God of all gods, loves us and wants this type of relationship with us.

However, despite how loving, all-sufficient, and gracious God is, many find it fitting to replace Him with other gods. If we find that God is not satisfying us enough so that we must go after other gods, then we not only offend Him, but we also damage ourselves.

God alone is to be worshipped, revered, and honored as Lord and King. The disasters the nation of Israel endured at the hands of Jehovah are strong re-minders of how deeply idolatry offends God. In God's dealings with Israel, He both exposed them and judged them harshly for their sin of idolatry.

We are prone to idolatry just like the people of Israel. Being born in sin and shaped in iniquity – idol-atry being one of them – our hearts often wonder away from the One we should adore to idols that seemingly satisfy us.

Israel, while under the leadership of Jeroboam, turned away from Yahweh to worship Baal. Although the people of Israel were God's chosen people and they enjoyed countless blessings from Him, they could not love Him with all their heart, soul, and strength. They could not wholly follow Him. Instead, they gave their allegiance to Baal and, as seen throughout the Scriptures, to many other gods. Elijah took this opportunity to expose the worthlessness of Baal and the futility and senselessness of idolatry. Elijah went to great lengths to prove to Israel that Yahweh was God.

In the showdown on Mount Carmel, Baal, the storm god, could not send fire down from heaven to ignite the altar. Yahweh, on the other hand, licked up the excess water that Elijah placed around the altar and consumed the sacrifice.

Yahweh is the God of the heavens and the earth. He controls the universe. Nothing is out of His reach because He created everything. He alone is God. He is the one and only true and living God; therefore, He alone is worthy of our worship.

Idols of Today

An idol is anything or anyone a person loves more than God, choose over God, desire more than God, cherish more than God, or enjoy more than God. Said differently, an idol is anything we give ourselves to, depend on, trust in, love, or place undue appreciation for or worth and value in. With this definition, we must understand that idols could be anything. They could be inherently harmful to us like illicit drugs, be a necessity, be good for us like education, our children or family, or our career. But they become idols when our sinful nature and greedy hearts twist and abuse them. Put succinctly, an idol is the creature that is esteemed above God the Creator; it could be anything that is created.

From the examples given, we see that idols are not always glaringly bad. In fact, the idols that many worship today are good, but as the Apostle Paul puts it:

> *All things are lawful unto me, but all things are not expedient: all things are lawful for me, but I will not be brought under the power of any.* – 1 Corinthians 6:12, KJV

These things may be harmless, but when we let them become our masters, we have now made them our gods. Although these things may be good, they may not be beneficial to us. They may be good but not best. The Apostle Paul says they are not expedient.

We must choose what's best. This places the demand on us to put everything and everyone in our lives in the right order of priority. Everything must be second to the one true God. None of these things should rule us. They must not dictate our emotions or our conduct. We must not set our affections on them. We must set our *"affections on things above, not on things on the earth"* (Colossians 3:2, KJV).

In Romans 1:25, the Apostle Paul says, "*They exchanged the truth about God for a lie and worshiped and served the creature.*" Everything that exists — visible and invisible, tangible, and intangible — were created. Therefore, when we worship the money earned from our jobs instead of Jehovah Jireh our provider or worship the items we buy with our earnings instead of God our provider, we grieve God with idolatry.

A question we could ask ourselves to determine if we are guilty of idolatry is: Is God number one in my life? And when answering this question, we must first be honest with ourselves and second, while pondering the response, give very careful thought to our conduct, interests, and lifestyle.

If we go to the biblical definition of idolatry, one could say idolatry is blatantly obvious and, therefore, is readily seen, but is that really the case? The verse says:

> *Put to death, therefore, whatever belongs to your earthly nature: sexual immorality, impurity, lust, evil desires and greed, which is idolatry.* – Colossians 3:5, NIV

Sexual immorality, impurity, lust, evil desires, and greed are often not hard to see. Therefore, one could say, based on the definition of idolatry given in this verse, idolatry is naked to the natural eye. But that is not always the case. If that were the case, I believe many who truly love the Lord but are tricked by the devil into idolatry would readily see it and resist it. But because it is not glaringly obvious, many believers are in idolatry and do not seem to know it.

The same writer, the Apostle Paul, gives another definition for idolatry. He says:

> Mortify therefore your members which are upon the earth; fornication, uncleanness, inordinate affection, evil concupiscence, and covetousness, which is idolatry. – Colossians 3:5, KJV

It is clearly stated here that covetousness is idolatry. Covetousness is not a deed of the body. It is not something we do that defines covetousness, it is a condition of the heart that is then followed with thoughts, words, and wrongful deeds. Covetousness, also referred to as idolatry by the Apostle Paul, starts in the heart. It starts with cravings, pleasures, desires, and self-satisfaction and being satisfied by anything that we treasure more than God.

Covetousness is displaced love and desire. It is loving and desiring something for ourselves more than we love God. This is what idolatry looks like today. For the most part, especially in the western world, not many people are bowing down before images and calling them their god.

The false gods we worship today are often not something we bow our knees to or offer sacrifices to like the Israelites did. In most cases, the things we worship are not even tangible, but they are gods or idols, nonetheless. The idolatry of today is mostly centered around us. We want for ourselves. We want pleasure, we want satisfaction, and society dictates that if we want it, we should get it. Thus, we live in a time when idolatry is thriving effortlessly, even among Christians. We live in an era when idolatry is not seen and responded to for what it is.

We live in an era where people across the globe — including followers of Jesus Christ — are more self-centered and individualistic than ever before. The baby boomer generation (born between 1946 and 1964) has been labeled "The Me Generation," and subsequent generations have seemingly grown progressively self-centered. Today, the commercials, the items that sell most, our lifestyle, and a host of other things point to the fact that we are preoccupied with ourselves. We have made gods out of ourselves.

I propose that the two things that point most to the current culture of self-centeredness are economic development and technology. These are the things that create the idols we tend to worship most, and I also propose that the idols of today mostly express themselves in three ways:

1. Individualism
2. Secularism
3. Narcissism

Leading Contributors to the Self-Centeredness of Today

Because of self-centeredness, our intellectual belief in the supremacy of God is not reflected in the way we live our lives. What we know does not line up with what we do. Our current times, especially those of us who live in the western world, are saturated with the Word of God and teachings about God. But this knowledge about God is not reflected in our priorities. We say and sing that we put God first, we say we give Him priority, but the truth is, we have other priorities and the main one is ourselves.

Going back to the impact of the cessation of corporate worship due to the COVID-19 pandemic on believers, misaligned priorities or failure to put God first is a good cause for spiritual decline and even cessation from attending church simply because the church doors were closed. If God is first in our lives, spiritual decline or church drop-out would not be the outcome whether the church doors are opened or closed.

I have identified economic development and technology as the two leading causes of the pervasion of self-centeredness of today.

Economic Development

Put differently, economic development is financial prosperity. Many today are living in the season of plenty. Some will not see it that way because greed has blurred their vision, and they are never satisfied. But if we compare today's lifestyle with that of our parents, grandparents, and beyond, we will quickly see that we are living a significantly more luxurious life than they ever did.

God wants us to thrive economically. He does not want His children to have unmet needs. He wants us to enjoy the wealth of His generosity toward us, but that does not mean we should feed the lusts of our flesh by getting what we want when we want it, even if it is by means of poor financial decisions.

Some common detrimental ramifications of wealth are pride and arrogance, a sense of self-sufficiency, complacency, and a false sense of security. With prosperity, we can become so comfortable that we have no sense of the subtlety of the enemy and how he works. Prosperity can make us careless and apathetic toward things of the Spirit. But often one does not even have to be wealthy to suffer the fate of these side-effects. Simply having a good income, being stable in one's career, and being able to spend as desired is enough to make some feel like they need no one, not even God.

One extreme example of this is recorded in Hosea 12:8, NET: "*I am very rich! I have become wealthy! In all that I have done to gain my wealth, no one can accuse me of any offense that is actually sinful.*" Here we see Ephraim boasting in his prosperity. We may not verbalize these words but our attitude toward God says it all.

Another example is Ezekiel's warning to the King of Tyre, who because of his wisdom in doing business, was proud due to the riches he had acquired: *"By all your wisdom in trade you have added to your riches, and your heart has become proud because of them"* (Ezekiel 28:5, NLV).

Complacency, self-sufficiency, and of course, this false sense of security are very dangerous to believers. Complacency gives no room for desiring more of God; it puts believers to sleep. It makes believers apathetic, full, and satisfied with their current state and their current spiritual surroundings. So, despite what is going on in and around them, they have no desire to pursue God. Complacent believers are stagnant; they do not grow. They are lukewarm, and God said He will spew such persons out of His mouth. To Him, they are revolting. This was the state of the Laodicean church.

Self-sufficiency and a false sense of security go hand in hand. You almost don't see one without the other. Because we live in a society that idolizes strength and independence, believers can easily fall prey to these seemingly good values. In this society, we are esteemed, and we gain the respect of others if we are high achievers and if we present with strength, competence, and capabilities. People admire these traits, and we want to be among the admired. While nothing is wrong with bearing these traits, we must know and live our lives like we know that none of this is possible without God.

The self-sufficient, like the Laodiceans, tell themselves they have no need for God or anyone else because they are trusting in the earthy treasures rather than the Creator and in heavenly treasures. This is a dangerously deceptive view, and that is what makes it so detrimental. It makes you feel as if you need nothing and that you know everything when in fact *"you are wretched and miserable and poor and blind and naked."*

> [16] *But since you are like lukewarm water, neither hot nor cold, I will spit you out of my mouth!* [17] *You say, 'I am rich. I have everything I want. I don't need a thing!' And you don't realize that you are wretched and miserable and poor and blind and naked.* –Revelation 3:16-17b, KJV

This was the state of the Laodiceans, and this is the state of the self-sufficient believers of today. With this mindset, we forfeit a great deal of spiritual growth potential. Man ought to be entirely reliant on God. Without dependence on God, we will never experience the peace and joy that await those who are totally dependent on Him.

Jesus, in His parable of the rich fool (Luke 12:13-21) warns against the danger of prosperity luring us into a false sense of security. Apparently, it is very easy to think that we have no need of God when our needs and wants are satisfied, when life is good, and when the future seems secure.

We should occupy until He comes (Luke 19:13b), and we should enjoy the fruit of our labor, but we should not self-indulge. Self-indulgence is a sin. Self-indulgence is excessive or unrestrained gratification of our appetites, desires, and wants. Doubtlessly, we will replace God with whatever we love most when we self-indulge.

Many today are guilty of self-indulgence simply because they have the financial means to do so. And even more sadly, some do not have the financial means but put themselves in financial distress just to keep pace with societal trends, like "get the latest and greatest," "you work hard so you deserve it," "if you want it, get it." Living in a society such as this ignites the flawed nature of man. So, we are all at risk of setting our affections on our possessions instead of God, but we must be reminded that when we do so, our number one is not God. This means our answer to the question, "Is God number one in your life?", is no...meaning, we have an idol.

Living in an age of plenty can also make us insensitive to the needs of others, making us callous and merciless. Jesus displayed this in the parable of the rich man and Lazarus in Luke 16:19-31. The rich man was enjoying his wealth and was totally oblivious of the needs of the poor man Lazarus. Although he had more than enough, he did not see or have any desire to address the plight of this poor man that sat at his gate.

The rich man was entirely absorbed in his lifestyle of prosperity and nothing else mattered.

This should not be the case, but unfortunately many are seduced by plenty or a comfortable lifestyle. Or many are going out of their way to obtain riches. Prosperity is a blessing, but it can be damaging. It is the gateway to doom for many. The taste of prosperity often opens the appetite for more. If the heart is not guarded, the prosperous will keep wanting more and more, and the more they have, the greater the risks for idolatry or divided affection. This won't work however, because God wants complete devotion to Him. He is jealous. He will not share us with another god.

Money is probably one of the most powerful distractions from God. We are told that the love of money is the root of, not some, but all evil (1 Timothy 6:10). This verse shows us the power that money has in dividing our loyalty and devotion to God. The Psalmist David knew this and alerted us when he wrote, "*If riches increase, set not your heart upon them*" (Psalm 62:10b, KJV). "*No one can serve two masters. Either you will hate the one and love the other, or you will be devoted to the one and despise the other. You cannot serve both God and money*" (Matthew 6:24, NIV).

It might be best to ask the Lord, "*Give me neither poverty nor riches, but give me only my daily bread. Otherwise, I may have too much and disown you and say, 'Who is the Lord?' Or I may become poor and steal, and so dishonor* the name of my Gods" (Proverbs 30:8-9, NIV). In this case, money or prosperity would not replace God.

Today it is quite easy to feed our greed whether we have the financial resources or not. We are bombarded with advertising; there is no getting away from it and advertising does its job. They tell us what we should buy, and they tell us how to get the credit to buy these things. Floyd Allen, an executive with General Motors, said it in a frank and honest way, "Advertising is the business of making people hopelessly dissatisfied with what they have in favor of something better." We buy and buy and hoard, but ironically, those who have plenty never seem to be satisfied. This state of dissatisfaction can lead to envy and covetousness as we compare what we have with that of others.

The environment in which we live has shaped us to believe that more is better, and more is not even enough. So, we are constantly desiring more things, more toys, the latest technology, and the high-end items. And these things — knowingly or unknowingly — replace God. Maybe this is what James was addressing when he wrote:

> [2] *You desire but do not have, so you kill. You covet but you cannot get what you want, so you quarrel and fight. You do not have because you do not ask God.* [3] *When you ask, you do not receive, because you ask with wrong motives, that you may spend*

what you get on your pleasures. — James 4:2-3, NIV

The Jewish Christians to which James was writing had strong desires for worldly things, not Yahweh. They were in the church, but their affection was not set on Yahweh. Could that be us today? Could that be the reason why some lost interest in church during the COVID-19 shutdown? Could it be because their affection was not on God before the shutdown, so not being able to go in the church building for corporate worship eliminated the one means by which they were maintaining?

Another effect of living with plenty is the tendency to worry. Not all of us are worry warts, but we are all prone to worry. However, because of the worth those who have plenty place on their possessions, contrary to what some may think, they can become anxious and full of worry about the future provision of their needs. Some are particularly anxious about having enough during their twilight years. The concern is whether they will have enough money to sustain them during this season of their lives.

This does not really make sense, and therefore, one would think that unsettling concerns about one's future would only be found among those who genuinely do not have enough to meet their needs. However, most people who have plenty also experience undue stress. Ironically, having more than enough to meet our needs seems to make us more anxious because now we have more possessions to lose.

Along with the insatiable desire for more, this unnecessary fear of not having enough is what drives some people to work multiple jobs and unnecessarily long hours, which often consume their time for corporate and personal spiritual development activities.

Note, this does not necessarily stop them from attending church or from being a Christian. They are members of the body of Christ but the efforts they place into securing their future provision displaces God, and is at the expense of serving Him wholeheartedly. These individuals have chosen church over God.

Technology

According to Techjury[17], over four billion people across the world actively use social media networks, mainly Facebook, Twitter, and Instagram. In April 2021, Pew Research Center reported that around 7 of every 10 Americans were using social media to connect with one another, engage with news content, share information, and entertain themselves. Pew Research Center began tracking social media use in 2005. At that time, a meager 5 percent of American adults were using at least one social media platform. By 2011, the usage rate was about 50 percent, in 2018, it was at 68 percent, and in 2021 it is 72 percent. These numbers tell us that social media is here to stay and that it in increasingly widely used, and the users are Christians and non-Christians alike.

The span of users is broad, and the amount of time spent on these platforms are equally extensive. As of 2020, the average daily social media usage of internet users worldwide amounted to 145 minutes (2 hours and 25 minutes) per day. The demographics of the study sample is unknown. Given the extensive hours that most teenagers and young adults in the western world spend on social media, it leaves one to wonder if these age groups were included in the sample.

According to GlobalWebIndex, Philippine residents lead the way with almost four hours (3 hours and 57 minutes) per day on social media platforms. Following them are the Brazilians with about three-and-a-half hours (3 hours and 39 minutes) per day. On the low end are the Japanese with only 48 minutes of social media time per day.

Technology is a great asset today and it is almost impossible to live without it. But like all good things, there are those who abuse it and have literally made it destructive. My mention of technology here is especially in reference to social media. Social media is an excellent tool in many ways. It can be a boon to individuals, ministries, and businesses, but it has a very covert dark side to which many Christians have fallen prey. For believers, it provides the perfect forum for idolatry in disguise.

Social media has its disadvantages, and it is a huge trap for many, but it is also very good. For example, it is an effective means of spreading the gospel. It is also an effective means of connecting with and encouraging other believers. It is effective in connecting with family and friends who are near and far — across the world, in different time zones, and in our backyards. It is through social media that many have reconnected with long-time friends and associates and have even located lost family members.

An immediate threat to Christians however is stolen time that could be spent doing things that are much more edifying, such as praying and reading the Bible or inspirational materials. Many can testify to the fact that it is quite easy to get on Facebook or Instagram, for example, for a quick check-in only to find themselves on there for hours. Others get caught up into the habit of checking their social media accounts first thing in the morning, throughout the day, and the last thing before going to bed at night but have not spent any time in prayer or the Word.

Something is wrong when anyone finds it necessary to give a weekly, daily, and sometimes multiple times per day account of what is happening in their lives. It calls for scrutiny when one finds it necessary to post every picture, mostly selfie of themselves on social media. Yes, you lost weight and you look good, but is it necessary to now dress yourself sparingly and post a whole lot of selfies? Who did you lose weight for — yourself or the public?

Yes, you are pregnant, and you are delighted. But is it necessary to share just about every intimate detail of the pregnancy journey? Is it necessary to share private matters between you and your spouse on social media? Sometimes it appears as if the line that divide private and public is blurred. These behaviors should not be found among believers. To whom are we drawing attention when we do these things? How does this bring glory to God?

What makes this worse is after each post these individuals anxiously wait for the "likes" to come in. They check frequently to see how many "likes" they get and from whom. And if they get few or no "likes," they're not happy. Who are the posts focused on? Why post these things for the "world" to see? Whose lives are these posts changing and how are they changing lives? Why are the "likes" important?

The "likes" are important because the society in which we live places much value and emphasis on looks and popularity. Therefore, "likes" indicate social acceptance, approval of looks and of popularity, and social acceptance is desirable. The world seeks it, and Christians are no exception. We want to be accepted and approved by the public as well. That is why we post and wait anxiously for the "likes." That is why we edit our photos before we post them to make them look better than we really look. That is why we post our best, be it true or not. That is why even when posting an announcement about an event or a worthwhile encouraging word, we place endearing pictures of ourselves along with the post that take away from the message. So, again, what is the purpose of these post? Are they to edify others or are they to attract attention to ourselves?

This is no different from preaching in the pulpit, for example. When we minister from the pulpit, we should never dress in such a way that attention is drawn from the message to us. We do just that when we post a worthwhile message on social media, but with the post, we include a picture of ourselves that draws the attention of the viewers from the message to us. We must examine why we do what we do and conclude that all we do should be for the glory of God our Father, never us.

If we answer the right questions — such as: Who are the posts focused on? Why post these things for the "world" to see? Whose lives are these posts changing and how are they changing lives? Why are the "likes" important? — honestly, we'll see that there is no edification in these self-centered posts. This is why I call this selfie and self-promotion era idolatry in disguise. We are idolizing ourselves and don't seem to know it.

The misuse of social media seems innocuous, but it has removed our attention from God to ourselves. We were already focused on ourselves but even more so now with that magic weapon called a "smart phone" in our hands. Why are people in the strangest places, for example, doctor's office, on the train, even in church pouching their lips, stroking their hair, and tilting their bodies in strange poses just to take a selfie? Why do they post every hairstyle, every outfit, their beautiful face after a make-up session, their newly arched eyebrows, their meals, their weight loss, their vacation pictures? Why? Do you see now how everything revolves around us? This is idolatry.

I was watching a service that was held at what we call a mega church on YouTube a couple years ago and what I saw was appalling and speaks very well to how social media has trapped up. The preacher made an altar call for the unsaved to receive Christ, and a young woman who was responding to the call saw it fit to film herself on Facebook live while she responded.

Where are the days of a broken spirit and a contrite heart? You see, people are more concerned about how they look, who sees them, and with posting videos that goes viral than they are with the essentials of life. This is what social media has drawn many into doing, and Christians are no exception.

Knowing or unknowingly, if you choose to publicize your life, you have created some unhealthy situations for you and for others. First, you position yourself to be dishonest with yourself and with those who are looking at you. You are dishonest because you only publish what seems to be good. By doing so, you are deceiving the viewers and are creating a scenario that wrongfully justifies a noteworthy level of social acceptance and approval. And worse, if things are not good, you pretend as if they are good.

Second, the massive volume of fake, good lives that are published on social media, to which you are contributing, perpetuates imitations, jealousy, covetousness, depression, and even suicide among viewers.

Third, and as mentioned above, this constant updating and posting of the events in your life directs all the focus on you.

It is Satan's desire to steal, kill, and destroy from us (John 10:10). Sadly, he has been far too successful at stealing, killing, and destroying many Christians' interests in the things of God. Instead, our interest is to find out what is going on in other people's lives or to go out of our way to portray a fake superficially happy life we wish we were living. Satan is quite fine distracting us from the superior. He's okay if we settle for the better, even the best, but we must aim for and settle for nothing less than the superior. God is the superior. Anything else is beneath that — worst, worse, poor, fair, good, better, best — are all beneath superior.

Expressions of Idolatry

Today, idolatry is expressed primarily in three ways: individualism, secularism, and narcissism.

Individualism

Individualism says, "I'm number one," "I've got to satisfy me," "I need to be happy." Notice the word that appears in all three statements: I. Individualism focuses on the person; other people don't matter at all or as much. Along with this comes a sense of rudeness and unfriendliness. I call it pride. The wise man Solomon warns that unfriendliness, selfishness, and contentiousness all go together. Therefore, if you bear any of these three characteristics, you will likely bear the other characteristics.

> *An unfriendly person pursues selfish ends and against all sound judgment starts quarrels.* – Proverbs 18:1, NIV

This explains why so many people of today's society are so inconsiderate and rude. And on top of that, no one can tell these individuals what to do. They refuse to hear godly counsel. The root is selfishness – self-centeredness – the idol we have created to worship in place of God.

Secularism

Secularism says, "God doesn't matter enough to be the head of my life." Most people in the world believe there is a God, but they don't make Him the object of their worship and devotion. They don't give Him place in their lives as the God that He is and wants to be to them. Some of these same people have the mindset that they don't need God, that is until tragedy hits. James 2:9b tells us that even demons believe that there is one God and shudder, but they are demons, nonetheless. They live and act like demons although they know the one true God exists. So, believing there is a living God is not enough. We must make Him the Lord of our lives.

Essentially, secularism acknowledges that God exists but chooses not to have anything to do with Him or chooses to involve Him, but only at their convenience. Job calls these people wicked (Job 21:14-17). They tell God to leave them alone. They don't want to know His will for their lives. They don't want to know His ways. In other words, they want to run their lives their way. In their mind, they can do it. This is secularism.

The psalmist David also called these people wicked. In Psalm 10:4 (NLT), he said, *"The wicked are too proud to seek God. They seem to think that God is dead."* This is very much like the people that Job referenced in chapter 21. These people do not give God the honor and reverence He deserves. They place Him lower than the highest place in their lives. To them, God is not number one.

If you recall, the question we must ask ourselves to determine if we are in idolatry or not is: Is God number one in my life? Clearly, from Scripture, we see that the answer that the people referenced by Job and by David would give to this question is no. But wait, let me caution you, do not think that these individuals are limited to the unregenerated. These people include the regenerated as well. It very likely will include Supplanters and Minimals, and potentially Church Lifers. So, can people who go to church become so full of themselves that they don't make God the head of their lives? The answer is an absolute yes.

Narcissism

Narcissism is gross self-centeredness. It says, "I'm all that matters!" Everything and everyone revolve around the narcissistic person. All energy, focus, and attention from these persons are on themselves, not anyone else, and definitely not God.

With economic development and a time of plenty or affluence comes a greater sense of self-reliance, indulgence, and detachment from others. This shift towards individualism puts us at risk of being less empathic — caring only about ourselves and our own welfare. We see that today, even in the church. People are becoming more isolated and focused on themselves rather than others. But we should not be surprised. The Bible tells us to expect this to happen in the last days:

> [1] *You should know this, Timothy, that in the last days there will be very difficult times.* [2] *For people will love only themselves and their money. They will be boastful and proud, scoffing at God,*

disobedient to their parents, and ungrateful. They will consider nothing sacred. – 2 Timothy 3:1-2, NLT

6

IDOLATRY ANSWERS THE QUESTION – CHURCH OR GOD?

When in idolatry, the person chooses whatever the focus of attention is over God. So, how does idolatry fit in the fabric of church? Isn't church supposed to be always about God? How could there be any element of idolatry in church if church is all about God? Isn't everything about church good?

We have established that the church is not the building; it is the people that come together to glorify God. The church is the bride of Christ, the people who have accepted Him as their Lord and Savior. But in this discussion, I will refer to church as the activities that occur within the buildings we often call church or the activities that are associated with church, also referred to as ministries. So, church in this discussion is weekly worship services, prayer meetings, conferences, mission trips, concerts, retreats, children's church, couples' ministry, singles' ministry, Lord's Supper or Communion, baptisms, fasting, family fun nights, preaching, teaching, counseling, singing / praise and worship, outreach, hospitality, and more.

These are all good and necessary things that all church ministries need to do. But while doing them, we must understand one main thing: it is the heart posture with which we do these things that really matters, not the activities themselves. While doing these good, church, religious things, we must do them with a heart of service and devotion to God. The focus must be on the Person, not the thing, the reputation of the church or ministry, not to make the pastor proud, and certainly, not on ourselves.

The moment our heart shifts from being fully focused on and devoted to God, as soon as these activities become anything but a heart sacrifice to an audience of one — God only — we have chosen church over God. Ministry activities have then become idols. We should be so devoted to God that though called to be a preacher, musician, worship leader, teacher, pastor, evangelist, prophet, or whatever the calling may be, we love Him more than and choose Him over these things. We know we have made ministry an idol when we prefer to do ministry than to spend time with Him in our secret place: time in prayer, His Word, and worship. Inversely, we know we have made God our number one when we would be at perfect peace if we are called to be a preacher, teacher, worship leader, missionary, or whatever the calling, but would choose spending quality time with Him over working the ministry.

Persons who have chosen church over God only study the Bible in preparation to teach or preach. Some don't even study the Bible under any circumstance, and that includes preachers and teachers. In this age of information overload, they can easily combine pieces of information from varying sources to compose a sermon or lesson. They are focused on ministry, and they love ministry activities, the thing, more than the Person, God. This is reflected in their neglect in spending quality time in the Word simply because they love the Lord and are seeking to know Him more deeply.

Another indicator of placing church over God is the obsession with being seen and recognized by others. The church is swarming with people who are desperate for attention. This is why people strive for titles and positions so much. This is unseemly for followers of Christ, but it is a subtle work of the flesh to which many have yielded. They have made self-glory more important to them than glorifying God. This is idolatry.

The individuals to whom titles are overly important are the ones who are sorely offended when not addressed by their titles, and this is the case whether they rightfully earn the title or not or whether they are living up to the title or not. Unfortunately, they forget or are totally unaware that the highest honor we could possibly receive is to be called a son (irrespective of gender) of God. Titles should be appropriately used and should be lived up to, but they are not necessary; it's our positional relationship with God that really matters.

Another example of seeking self-glory that is quite prevalent in the church is the use of multiple titles when addressing a person. I believe we take our eyes off the One who is to receive all the honor when anyone addresses themself as or allow others to address them with multiple titles simultaneously, for example, doctor, bishop, apostle, and prophet. Why are all these titles necessary in one sentence when addressing one person? How many honors does one person need? It begs the question as to what these individuals are trying to convey or achieve for themselves when they refer to themselves or allow others to address them as such.

Whenever you hear anyone being addressed with multiple titles at the same time, it is blatantly obvious that these individuals have chosen self-image and self-reputation over God. This is an attention-seeking behavior. It is an attempt to get the glory and admiration that belongs to God, and sadly, it seems to be working. This overloading of titles and accolades often take place while in the house of the Lord. We are so bent on esteeming ourselves that in seeking to satisfy the flesh, we lose respect for God and His house. This is idolatry.

If nowhere else, the Lord is to be honored in His house, but we rob God of His glory even while in

His house. All the glory belongs to Him, and we must keep in mind, that small glory or big glory, it is His. No matter who we are or who we think we are, we should never draw attention to ourselves.

Yes, we must honor those that serve in ministry. They should be respected, but self-driven attempts to glorify oneself should not have any place in ministry. The mantra of every follower of Christ should be "I decrease, and Christ increases" and "None of me and all of You." There are no stars or superstars in Christendom. It is a privilege and an honor that God choose any of us for use in ministry, no matter what that task is. The desire to be known, viewed as distinguished, and lifted up by man is an obvious indication that we have chosen church over God. The idol called self that we have created has displaced God. This is idolatry.

We must remember that when Jesus calls, His immediate command is that we follow Him. He does not call and immediately assigns to ministry. In Matthew 4:19 (KJV) when Jesus called Peter and Andrew, He said to them, "*Follow Me, and I will make you fishers of men.*" Follow me first, then I will make you an evangelist. We must make Jesus our priority, then ministry will follow. We must seek Him first and His righteousness (Matthew 6:33), then ministry will fall in line as it should.

God wants us to love Him. He wants us to keep Him as the reason for everything we do in ministry. He felt this way about His chosen people, the nation of

Israel and He feels no differently about us today. Thus, God said this to His people through the prophet Hosea:

> I want you to show love, not offer sacrifices. I want you to know me more than I want burnt offerings. –Hosea 6:6, NLT

God wants us to love Him first and then He will work through us to work the ministry to His glory. He wants us to seek Him — the Giver not the gift — first. This is more important to Him than us seeking to be used by Him in ministry or to perfect ministry. He wants us to know Him. He wants to share His heart with us. He wants to confide in us and make His covenant known to us (Psalm 24:14). He wants us to be so close to Him that He can share His secrets with us. As seen in Amos 3:7 (NIV), God wants to reveal things to us before He does them. *Surely the Sovereign Lord does nothing without revealing His plan to His servants the prophets.*

But when we put anything, even ministry or any good deed, before Him, we grieve Him. We distance ourselves from Him and we remove the opportunity for Him to reveal His heart to us when we put anything above Him. He wants a relationship with us first, then we can work with Him, not for Him; then He can work through us.

Earlier, I talked about four groups of church goers: Relationals, Church Lifers, Supplanters, and

Minimals. Church Lifers are at highest risk for losing focus and making an idol out of church and its associated activities, and church or ministry idols are probably the hardest to detect because those deeds are good. Those activities are not glaringly wrong, so it is easy to think all is well and God is glorified.

For example, the worship leaders who are more concerned about making sure the people have a good time, making sure they sing the most popular or loved songs, making sure their performance and the sound of the music is spot on, and that they have the best musicians and singers, have lost focus. These musicians have made the activity the focus not the One to whom the activity is to be an offering.

We should never give anything but the best to God, but the first thing we must ensure is "best" is our hearts. If our hearts are "best," the offering we give to Him will naturally be best. So, instead of preparing their hearts to offer a sacrifice of praise to the King of kings, the worship leaders who have made the activity their focus, have created an idol out of the ministry of leading God's people into worship, and has therefore put the ministry activity above God. They have chosen church over God. This is typical of the church of Thyatira — good works but no spiritual power.

But one could easily overlook this act of idolatry. The pastor could highly appreciate those type of worship leaders because they demonstrate that they want to do such a good job. But what is the motive? Is it to give God the best? Is it to evoke the presence of God so that the Holy Spirit can freely work among the people? Is it to make sure people walk away from the worship service, saying the worship leader did an awesome job and is preferred above other worship leaders? These behaviors are hard or see with the naked eyes, but God sees them, and He is deeply grieved.

Another example is the believers who are immersed in the formalities of church — Church Lifers. I am in no way saying we should sloppily put things together and call it church, but when we focus more on the logistics than on the spiritual effectiveness of what we do, we've lost focus. These are the individuals who felt lost when churches could not meet for worship. Because they thrive in the church environment and the formalities of church instead of through a direct connection with God, they were out of place when church gatherings were not permitted. They were removed from their spiritual lifeline, and because they have limited personal spiritual enrichment discipline, these individuals will likely decline spiritually during the shutdown.

The pastors who refused to close the church doors or the ones who struggled while the doors were closed and could not wait to go back to "church as usual" could very well have placed church over God. Pastors who could not make the temporary adjustment to serve the people outside the four walls of the church may have chosen church over God. Believers who felt lost because they could not go inside a church building to do "church as usual" may have chosen church over God.

We have chosen church over God when we are wedded to the church program — Bible class, praise and worship, a sermon, altar call, then the dismissal or some variation of that. When we cannot divert from the program and have the assurance that we can still experience God, we have placed church over God. When we cannot find God and experience Him on our own or in the privacy of our homes away from the church building and other believers, we have placed church over God.

Because church and its logistics — titles, attire, protocol, routine, programs, structure, church rules, order — are the focus, many do not even realize that God, the Holy Spirit, has left their gatherings. They are having Bible studies and worship services, conferences, and all sort of church activities, but God is not there, and no one seems to know. This reminds me of what I call the saddest verse in the Bible:

> Then she called, "Samson, the Philistines are upon you!" He awoke from his sleep and thought, "I'll go out as before and shake myself free." But he did not know that the Lord had left him. — Judges 16:20, NIV

Many shake themselves in the form of doing ministry because they have been doing it for years, but the Lord has left them, and they don't know it. Samson shook himself many times and great strength came forth. But this time, his strength, the Lord, had left him and he did not know it. Preachers, teachers, worship leaders, missionaries, and many others in ministry have done the same. Like Samson, God will leave us if we entertain idols. This is a sad and very dangerous place to be.

If the focus is so much on something or someone else in the very house where God is to be praised and glorified, the place where He should be the center of attention, why should He stay? Or if the focus is on someone or something else when taking care of His business, why should He keep doing business with us? We should know that we would have no ministry if there was no God — so ministry should be all about Him. Therefore, if we take His business and desecrate it with selfish motives, why should He still partner with us? This kind of conduct gives Him the right to take His business elsewhere. He has done so, and many in ministry are totally oblivious to the fact that He has left.

This is why sinners, the sick, the emotionally broken, those bound by sin, the oppressed, and the depressed attend many church services week after week and leave the same. And the situation worsens because no one seems to notice, and no one seems to be bothered by the ineffectiveness of the ministry. We know that we have chosen church over God when the absence of the supernatural move of God does not arouse us to seek God for more.

Some have been going to church for so long that church activities have become what they do. These religious activities are what they do but God fades in the background. So, they engage in the activities without meaning. Their heart is not in it, and they are not looking for God in what they do. Therefore, they are not concerned by the lack of results from their ministry or church activities. It is enough to have church. It is good enough to do church ministries as usual: get the people in the building, execute the program, observe the ceremonies, get these things done because this is church, and they should be done and that's it. That is putting church over God.

People with this mindset feel out of place if they don't engage in church activities, but it is not because they want to worship God; it is because these church activities have become routine and, often unknowing to them, are placed above God. Without these activities, as routine as they are, these people do not feel like Christians. The children of Israel were like that. It got to the point where God told them He no longer wanted their sacrifices.

> [21] *This is what the Lord of Heaven's Armies, the God of Israel, says: "Take your burnt offerings and your other sacrifices and eat them yourselves!* [22] *When I led your ancestors out of Egypt, it was*

not burnt offerings and sacrifices I wanted from them. [23] This is what I told them: 'Obey me, and I will be your God, and you will be my people. Do everything as I say, and all will be well!' – Jeremiah 17:21-23, NLT

[10] Listen to the Lord, you leaders of "Sodom." Listen to the law of our God, people of "Gomorrah." [11] "What makes you think I want all your sacrifices?" says the Lord. "I am sick of your burnt offerings of rams and the fat of fattened cattle. I get no pleasure from the blood of bulls and lambs and goats. [12] When you come to worship me, who asked you to parade through my courts with all your ceremony? [13] Stop bringing me your meaningless gifts; the incense of your offerings disgusts me! As for your celebrations of the new moon and the Sabbath and your special days for fasting – they are all sinful and false. I want no more of your pious meetings. – Isaiah 1:10-13, NLT

So, we can be devoted church goers, have multiple titles, be preachers, be teachers, be lay members, or be anything in the church and have placed church (the thing) over God (the Person). This is idolatry.

Idols can only make promises; they cannot keep them. But we foolishly create idols and believe they can fulfil their seductive promises. We believe money can secure our happiness and joy. We believe pleasure can be our refuge and comfort. We believe success in business will validate our worth. We believe successful children will equate with our success. We believe religion can save us. But idols will fail us, and they separate us from God. Replacing the one true God with an idol is as foolish as worshipping Baal, and we see what happened to the Baal worshippers.

God must be our object of love and trust, not ministry. There shouldn't be anything we love more than we love God. We must know that only God can truly secure and satisfy us.

God is after our hearts. He wants our full devotion and worship, and He deserves our deepest and strongest affections.

Although common, idolatry is a serious problem. If the greatest commandment is to *"love the Lord your God with all your heart, all your soul, and all your mind"* (Matthew 22:37, NLT), then idols can become our "greatest sin." Idolatry clouds our thinking, distracts our focus, and ultimately keeps us from glorifying God.

7

THE MARRIAGE RELATIONSHIP

Ephesians 5:31 is a quotation of Genesis 2:24, which says, "*For this reason a man shall leave his father and mother and be joined to his wife, and the two shall become one.*" The Apostle Paul then added this in Ephesians 5:32, "*This is a great mystery, and I take it to mean Christ and the church.*" Paul is saying that the concept of a man leaving his parents and being joined to the woman he loves to become one is a mystery. He is also saying that the full understanding of how two people can become one is hidden; that is why he refers to it as a mystery. He points out that the whole discussion of marriage between a man and a woman is symbolic of the marriage between Christ and His bride.

As described in Genesis 2:24, marriage is the union of a man and a woman into oneness. This is a mystery because the truth that the whole concept of marriage conveys about Christ and the church is not openly conveyed or readily understood. Just like the teachings of Jesus were hidden in parables, so is the union between Christ and the church hidden in the description of marriage between a man and a woman.

The true meaning that is hidden in the metaphor of marriage is that as seen in the scripture below, God established an unbreakable union between His Son, Jesus, and the church, His bride. From a corporate and individual level, all born-again believers must live with the understanding that God has married us. He is our husband.

> For I am jealous over you with godly jealousy: for I have espoused you to one husband, that I may present you as a chaste virgin to Christ. – 2 Corinthians 11:2, KJV

Geoffrey Bromiley puts the concept that marriage between a man and a woman is the earthly expression of God's marvelous plan for the church this way: "As God made man in His own image, so He made earthly marriage in the image of His own eternal marriage with His people".[18]

In Judaism, marriage is a solemn bond between two people; it is a sacred, binding agreement. Marriage is marked by both partners – the man and the woman – committing themselves to each other only, no one else, and they make this pledge to be faithful and loyal to one another publicly.

Like a wedding ceremony is a display of the couple's unending love and devotion to one another, so is baptism a display of our devotion to Christ. Weddings are a display of love and commitment and should not be done in secret. Wedding ceremonies are a public display that the partners are no longer available for a relationship with anyone but their spouse. Similarly, baptisms should be done publicly to tell the world that we pledge allegiance to Christ alone.

Earthly Versus Spiritual Marriage

In addition to a required public ceremony — meaning there must be witnesses — there are a lot of other similarities between earthly and spiritual marriages. But the first thing I want to point out about marriages — earthly and spiritual — is they require vows. A marriage ceremony is not complete without vows. This is where the parties express their commitment to each other and, in a lot of cases, their belief in each other. A vow is a sacred promise. It is not to be taken lightly. By all means, vows are to be upheld.

We see mutual vows at earthly marriage ceremonies all the time, and one may think that is not the case for spiritual marriages, but it is no different in a spiritual marriage. We make a vow to the Lord, our spiritual spouse, and He does the same. As seen in Deuteronomy 28:9 (NIV), the Lord made an oath to His chosen people: "*The Lord will establish you as his holy people, as he promised you on oath, if you keep the commands of the Lord your God and walk in obedience to him.*" Another can be found in Ezekiel 16:59 (NLT): "*Yet I will remember the covenant I made with you when you were young, and I will establish an everlasting covenant with you."* These are two of many accounts of the Lord expressing His devotion and faithfulness to His bride.

Earthly marriages generally involve a period of dating, engagement, ceremony, celebration, the sharing of love, and legal responsibility. Earthly marriage was ordained by God, so it was meant to be beautiful. But it is also challenging, requiring daily attention. It only takes one partner in a marriage relationship to become slightly distracted or neglectful in connecting with their spouse for a declining marriage, marked by complacency or discord, to emerge.

Spiritual marriage is just what it says: a spiritual connection. There are no physical elements to this marriage relationship. Our spiritual spouse is not physical, and He does not operate in the physical realm. Spiritual marriage is a commitment of the highest divine nature — spirit to spirit.

Other similarities between earthly and spiritual marriages are:

Love for Your Spouse

Love is the number one element in any marriage relationship. The Word of God says, *"Husbands, love your wives, even as Christ also loved the church"* (Ephesians 5:25, KJV). If love is present in the marriage, all the other factors listed below as elements of earthly and spiritual marriages will be present. Love will make you want to know your spouse, want to spend time with him/her, want to be in his/her company, work hard at keeping the marriage healthy, and will do the needful to improve the relationship when there are any signs of decline.

Additionally, love will make it easy for you to make personal changes, adjustments, and sacrifices just to please your spouse and to make the relationship work. Therefore, in our relationship with the Lord, we must be prepared and willing to make personal adjustments so that our ways will please Him. If we are to have a strong relationship with the Lord, we must know that personal sacrifices are required of us.

This means we will need to give up some of the ways of doing things that we hold dear to our hearts. Some of these things may be so deeply engrained that they define us. We must be ready to give up some things that require deep inner changes, and if we love the Lord, we will allow Him to work in and through us to make these changes. The beauty here, that is usually not present in earthly marriages, is that the Lord helps us make these difficult personal changes. We cannot make these changes without His help. He gives us the grace and strength to do so. Our earthly spouses cannot do that.

Know Your Spouse

The "*know*" that I'm talking about is not to know *about* the person, it is to *know* the person. That is, to know how they think, what they like and do not like, their interests, their desires, and other invisible and intangible things about them. A succinct word for this knowing is intimacy. I've seen intimacy interpreted as into-me-see, and I cannot help but agree. This level of knowing looks beyond the obvious into the person.

To *know* the Lord is to know His heart, it's to have a mind like His (Philippians 2:5), and it's to know His character. This goes beyond reading or hearing about God from others. We must have our own personal experiences with Him which will expose us to the various dimensions of His character and will in turn result in a progressive personal relationship with Him.

To know the Lord, we must spend time in His Word. We cannot separate the Word of God from God Himself, so when we read and study His Word, we are spending time with Him. When we read His Word, He is speaking to us. The Word of God will show us who He is. This is where we learn best about His nature, His character. The reading of His Word creates opportunities for encounters and personal experiences with Him, and we get to know Him more deeply after each encounter.

Also, to know the Lord, we must spend time in prayer and private worship. While praying with other believers has its place and should be a standing practice for all believers, the prayer time referenced here is pointing to private time with the Lord. The key word here is private. Remember, this is between you and your spouse. These are efforts to build your marriage relationship, so they should not be done with a third party. Intimate activities in an earthly marriage should involve the two partners only, no third party. These activities should be done in the privacy of your inner chamber. In a spiritual marriage, these activities should be done in our prayer closet, our secret place.

In the Bible, whenever reference is made that a man "knew" his wife, there was always a child, some fruit, a product from the "knowing" experience. An example:

> [1] *And Adam knew Eve his wife; and she conceived, and bare Cain, and said, I have gotten a man from the Lord.* [25] *And Adam knew his wife again; and she bare a son, and called his name Seth: For God, said she, hath appointed me another seed instead of Abel, whom Cain slew.* – Genesis 4:1, 25, KJV

Similarly, when we *know* the Lord, we bear spiritual fruit. We should have something to show for our knowing Him. But if we don't know Him in the sense I am discussing here, we will be fruitless. Jesus Himself said so:

> *Abide in me, and I in you. As the branch cannot bear fruit of itself, except it abide in the vine; no more can ye, except ye abide in me.* – John 15:4, KJV

Spend Time with Your Spouse

Time spent with your spouse must be a priority. You cannot be married, yet you spend most of your time with others. Your spouse will begin to think you have other lovers. Your spouse will think you're cheating on them or they'll think you simply aren't ready for marriage or are serious about the relationship.

It begs to question a person's commitment to a relationship when they choose to spend their time with others over their spouse. Therefore, as Christians – the bride of Christ – when we choose to do everything except spend quality private time with Jesus our Savior, the lover of our souls, it may very well be because we have other lovers. We may very well be guilty of spiritual adultery.

Colossians 3:2 (KJV) says, "*Set your affection on things above, not on things on the earth.*" Therefore, in a spiritual marriage, we must love the things of God. We should find the highest degree of pleasure in the things that pertain to God, and if that is the case, that is where we will spend our time, talent, and treasure (our money) most. I agree with the person that said if anyone wants to know what a person loves, they should look in their checkbook. People aren't writing a lot of checks these days, but you can look at their bank and credit card statements to see where their heart lies. Matthew 6:21 (KJV) validates this: "*For where your treasure is, there will your heart be also.*"

Our worth to God in public is measured by what we really are in our private lives. So, if we do not have a private prayer life or a disciplined private time for reading and meditation upon the Word of God, we will be of no use to Him in public. Many of us want to have powerful public ministries without spending time with Him, but that is entirely unrealistic. We want to operate under the anointing of the Holy Spirit without spending quality time with Him, but that will not happen. This is one of the prices we pay for the anointing. I strongly believe in this saying: salvation is free, but the anointing will cost you. One way we pay is with sacrificial time spent with Him so that we can know Him and have a meaningful relationship with Him. Out of that relationship will flow the working of the ministry, be it public or private.

Enjoy Your Spouse's Company

The degree to which you spend time with your spouse reflects how much you enjoy your spouse's company. Same thing with the Lord. The amount of time we spend in His presence — and I'm speaking mostly of private time — reflects the degree to which we enjoy being with Him. We can do a host of things while in His presence. We can let Him talk to us by listening to or reading His Word, pray, sing/worship, declare His Word over situations, meditate, or journal, and all these things are expressions of our love and desire for Him.

Our desire for and the priority we place on being in the assembly of the saints or fellowshipping with the saints, whether in church gatherings or small group settings are important but to a lesser degree. Attending corporate worship services and fellowshipping with the saints are also reflections of the joy we find in spending time with Him, but it cannot be compared with the expressions of love for the Lord shown in a life that is marked by a delight in private quality time with Him.

This walk with the Lord is a relationship between us and Him, and quality time is essential to all relationships. The Lord wants us to *know* Him, love Him, and desire Him above anything and anyone else. And one of the best ways to show we love someone is to simply love being in their presence. It is no different with God.

Our Lord not only wants us to spend time with Him but He also wants to spend time with us. He loves us and He wants to commune with us. He wants to share His heart with us, and as believers, we should want to know His heart more than anything else. Don't you want to know what makes Him smile or what gives Him delight in you? Don't you want to know what He loves and what He hates? Don't you want to involve Him in the most minute affairs of your life? Don't you want to know the little things about you that makes Him proud of you? Usually, children want their father to be proud of them. It should be no different with God our Father.

Scripture tells us that if we draw nigh to Him, He will draw nigh to us (James 4:8). If we seek Him, we will find Him (Jeremiah 29:13). He wants us to come close to Him. He wants us to seek Him, and He wants us to find Him. The fact that He tells us to seek Him, indicates that He is not always right there in plain sight. In other words, He is saying if you want Me bad enough, look for Me. Look for Me until you find Me. Love and a desire for Him will make us seek Him.

When seeking for something, we pursue it. We look everywhere; that includes places we least expect it to be. So, we don't just look in one place and then stop. Because finding God is not a one-time effort, He makes sure the seeking is an evolving process in our walk with Him; He makes it an adventure. He is such a mysterious and multifaceted God that every time we discover something about Him, it opens another level of hunger in us for Him, simply because He is inexhaustible. This makes the seeking a life-long venture. We will never fully discover God. That is the seeking, and it is a joyous experience to get to know the Lord at a deeper level after every encounter, after every revelation from Him.

Here are two verses that show us that God wants to spend time with us:

Does a young woman forget her jewelry, or a bride her wedding dress? Yet for years on end my people have forgotten me. — Jeremiah 2:32, NLT

Come close to God, and God will come close to you. Wash your hands, you sinners; purify your hearts, for your loyalty is divided between God and the world. – James 4:8, NLT

Seek to Make Your Spouse Happy

To make our earthly or spiritual spouses happy, we must know what they like. We must know what brings them joy. This brings us back to the point made earlier that we must know the Lord and we must find joy in spending time with Him. The more we spend time with the Lord, the more deeply we will know Him.

All the other things I have mentioned about spiritual marriage are important, but this one is very important because the one word that describes pleasing God, or making Him happy, is obedience. God honors obedience. In God's system of operation, blessings are associated with obedience and curses are linked with disobedience. We get His attention when we try to obey Him. He dispatches help from heaven when He sees us trying to obey Him. He has told us that His grace is all we need, it is sufficient, and that His power works best in our weakness (2 Corinthians 12:9), so help is available to us to enable us to obey Him.

Our obligation as the bride of Christ is to bring Him pleasure, so we should aim to put and keep a smile on His face. He created all things to give Him pleasure and that includes us (Revelation 4:11). Hence, our goal should be to please Him: *"So whether we are here in this body or away from this body, our goal is to please him"* (2 Corinthians 5:9, NLT).

As the bride of Christ, obedience to God should be our way of living, meaning obedience is a recurring act; it's our pattern of behavior. We should obey Him in good and bad circumstances and even in the most minor decisions of life. By obeying our Lord and Savior, especially when it is our way of life, we tell Him we love and trust Him.

Obedience is God's love language so there is no better way to tell Him we love Him than to obey Him. Two verses that convey this about God are:

> *If you love me, obey my commandments.* – John 14:15, NLT

> *What is more pleasing to the Lord: your burnt offerings and sacrifices or your obedience to his voice? Listen! Obedience is better than sacrifice, and submission is better than offering the fat of rams.* –1 Samuel 15:22, NLT

Work at the Marriage Daily to Keep It Alive

Believing in God is one thing; having a relationship with Him is another. Just like a marriage, having an intimate relationship with God requires daily effort and time. To have such a relationship, it is of utmost importance to interact daily with your earthly spouse and so it is with the Lord. Going days on end without talking to your spouse or with God will create distance between the parties.

Also, living our lives as believers without being tuned in to our conduct, our words, our attitude, or our thoughts will cost us spiritually. The wise King Solomon tells us in Proverbs 4:23 to guard our heart with all diligence. We ought to guard our hearts above all else. We must watch out for and filter out what goes through the gates of our ears and eyes and into our hearts, and we must do this with diligence, meaning we must do so with persistence, conscientiousness, and watchfulness. We cannot take a break from guarding our hearts. This is a significant means by which we work at our relationship with the Lord daily.

If we are not intentional about how we live, we will naturally — without effort — live out our own will and agendas, not God's. This is human nature. As believers, we all know — at least intellectually — that it is unwise and futile to live for the things of this world. We know that these vain things, the idols we pursue, promise satisfaction and peace, but they do not deliver. We know that true peace and joy can only be found in God, but somehow, we rest long enough, we drop our guard sufficient for the love of the world to seep into our hearts.

This is one reason we see so much worldliness in the church. Many of us drop our guard. We become tolerant of and less sensitive to the things of the world because we do not guard our hearts diligently. This comes at a very high price because we are told clearly in that being friends with the world makes us an enemy of God (James 4:4). We cannot be friends or in a relationship with God while being friends with the world.

The formula to break ties with the world and settle into a faith relationship with the Lord is in Romans 12:2 (NLT):

> *Don't copy the behavior and customs of this world, but let God transform you into a new person by changing the way you think. Then you will learn to know God's will for you, which is good and pleasing and perfect.*

For God to change the way we think, we must guard our hearts. Jesus taught that it is what comes in our bodies that defiles us (Matthew 15:11), and we should know that what comes out of our bodies depends solely on what goes in it. Therefore, we must, by all means, filter what goes in our hearts. We cannot allow the lies of the enemy to enter our hearts (or minds). Neither can we allow the systems of the world to find a place in our way of thinking.

If we are to guard our hearts with all diligence, we can never rest. We must always be on guard. So not only a day but not even a moment should go by without us working to keep our spiritual marriage alive and well.

Make Sacrifices to Keep the Marriage Alive

There is an inevitable demand for change when two people come together to be one. In an earthly marriage, two people from two different worlds with different up-bringings, habits, preferences, and ways of doing things are expected to live in harmony as one unit. Both parties must make some personal sacrifices for the marriage to work.

Likewise, when in relationship with the Lord, we must make some sacrifices. God is flawless and absolute, so He has no need to make any changes for the relationship to work. In this relationship, the demand for change is on us.

An unnegotiable essential for this change is submission, and the party that must submit in this relationship is us, certainly not God. A submitted life will create a place of habitation for God in our lives and in our hearts. And He should not only hold a place of habitation, but He should be established as Lord of our lives, meaning He is at the highest place in our lives.

God will not dwell in a place that is sinful. We must make sacrifices to create a place of habitation for the Spirit of Christ. For Christ to sit upon the throne of our hearts, we must make some adjustments, most of which will require a private, painful process. In other words, we must change our ways to be more like Christ.

For example, change is required if we tend to belligerently confront others without hesitation, and when doing so, our sole concern is to say what's on our minds without concern for how the person feels. Behaviors of this nature will not reflect the beauty of Christ and must be changed. Perhaps this is a common behavior pattern in your family; meaning it is a learned behavior. These kinds of behaviors that are engrained in us are difficult to change, but if Christ is truly going to be the Lord and ruler of our lives, we must give up some things, even the dearest things to us that do not please Him.

We must make this personal sacrifice and surrender our ways that are unseemly to Christ so that our relationship with Him can grow deeper and more intimate. But no one makes this kind of personality adjustment in one attempt, neither can anyone make such a change without the help of the Holy Spirit. This kind of inner change is often a painful, private process with lots of failures before seeing any change, but because of our love for God, we allow Him to do the necessary work in us.

We should know that the more time we spend with God, the closer we get to Him and Him to us, and the closer He gets to us, the more He will show us things about us that do not please Him. But we are to draw nigh to Him anyhow. We are to come to Him just as we are, but we should not stay as we are. For all believers, spiritual growth and becoming more like Christ is a must.

God demands change, so, some of the things He shows us will be modes of conduct and thought patterns that are embedded in us. Some are generationally learned behaviors that are near impossible to unlearn on our own. These are changes that require noteworthy personality adjustments, thus the sacrifice, but the payoff is much greater than the sacrifices we make.

Making these sacrifices becomes easier when we submit to God. James tells us the same: *"Submit yourselves therefore to God. Resist the devil, and he will flee from you"* (James 4:7, KJV). An unconditional yes, a total surrender, and the willingness for Him to do what only He can do to make us more like Him is an absolute necessity to build and maintain a close relationship with the Lord.

When the Marriage Is Waning, Make the Extra Effort to Revive It

Every marriage — earthly and spiritual — will be challenged and will experience cold spells. The appropriate thing to do for the wellbeing of the relationship is to address the issue. Do not ignore the fact that the relationship is declining. In earthly marriages, couples take weekends away. They may go to a couples' retreat; some go to couples' therapy. Sometimes, one partner creates a romantic evening with special treats just to rekindle the fire.

The very same applies to our relationship with the Lord. It is to our detriment if we do nothing when we see that our passion or hunger for the Lord is dissipating. We must do everything under the leading of the Holy Spirit to draw close to the Lord. First, if we sin, we must tell God we have sinned, and He alone can and will forgive us. In 1 John 1:9 (NLT), we read, *"If we confess our sins to him, he is faithful and just to forgive us our sins and to cleanse us from all wickedness."*

To get back to and beyond our place with the Lord, we may need to fast, maybe engage in a small group study, go back to reading the Bible regularly, seek guidance from a more mature believer, pray regularly and more deeply, or rebuild our altar in our homes and rekindle the fire there. Sometimes we need to change our company —our friends —and our social outlets. Any number of things can be done to restore and enhance our relationship with the Lord.

Relationships necessitate work, and so does this one. So, we cannot do nothing and expect a close relationship with the Lord. By doing nothing, we create an open door for the enemy of our souls to come in sow tares.

Marriage Expectations

It goes without saying that when people marry, they expect their spouse to spend time with them, love them, and be devoted to them. It wouldn't be okay if the spouse devotes more time with or gives more attention to others. Because they are in a covenant relationship, there should be no competition with others for attention. So, an inherent expectation is total devotion, no other lovers, no idols.

God freed His people from being slaves to the Egyptians, and in return, He expected them to love and serve Him. This is where the Ten Commandments came into being, and the very first one addresses this issue: *"Thou shalt have no other gods before me"* (Exodus 20:3, KJV). Could it be that of ten commandments, God chose to dictate this one first because it is of most importance to Him?

And note, the second commandment instructed them to not make and bow down to any images or idols. God was clear. He wanted all their worship. God expected total devotion. He demanded complete faithfulness to Him. He commanded them to follow His ways and worship only Him.

In our marriage relationship with God, He expects us to be devoted to Him alone. Having other gods is displeasing to Him, and in His eyes, it is adultery. When we choose to worship idols, we are like a wife who cheats on her husband.

More than anything, God wants to call us His own. Just before God delivered His people from Egypt, He said, *"I will claim you as my own people, and I will be your God. Then you will know that I am the Lord your God who has freed you from your oppression in Egypt"* (Exodus 6:7, NLT). God is referring to the nation of Israel, but this is pertinent to all who accepts Him as their God.

We have been freed from our own Egypt, a life-style of sin, and God expects the very same thing from us — total devotion. We are to worship Him only. There should be no gods or idols in our lives. We should be set apart for Him alone. This is a basic expectation of the spiritual marriage.

Once we accept Jesus as our Lord and Savior, we should live our lives with the knowledge and understanding that, ultimately, we were created for such an intimate union with God. We were born for this. Christ died and rose again to give us access to this union with Him and God the Father. God is high and holy. He is the exalted, most lofty One, yet He desires a relationship with us. This is one of the great mysteries of God and we should be delighted to be a part of it.

8

HE WANTS IT ALL

God is very clear that we are to have no other gods; we are to bow down to Him only. He goes on to say His very name is Jealous (Exodus 34:14). So, jealousy is one of His characteristics. How is this not self-centered? Is God's demand for total devotion selfish or narcissistic?

Here lies one of the beauties of God. His passion for us to adore and love Him is an expression of His love for us. Consider how far removed we are from Him. Consider how pure and holy He is and how downright sinful and filthy we are, how flawed we are and how perfect He is, yet He longs to fellowship with us. This is pure unconditional love, the direct opposite of narcissism. He knows man is nothing without Him, so He urges us to serve Him and Him only. Our best interests are His. His thoughts toward us are good (Jeremiah 29:11).

This is for our good, not His. Therefore, His desire is to draw us to Him with His relentless love and break our bondage to the idol of self and focus our affections on the treasures in Him. God is God with and without us and our worship. God is not weak, and He has no deficiencies: *"For everything comes from him and exists by his power and is intended for his glory. All glory to him forever!"* (Romans 11:36, NLT). He is God no matter what, but He is worthy of our praise through a devoted life.

All creation exists because of God. Everything, everyone, and anything now and to come owes its being to God. God is complete. No one and nothing can add anything to Him. He is the eternal God from whom all blessings flow. Therefore, God's desire to fellowship with us through complete devotion, praise, and worship from us is in no way to validate Him as God or to compensate for any deficiency.

Although He desires our praise, it is interesting that God does not wait for us to exalt Him. He took the initiative from the beginning of times to exalt His own name in the earth and to display His glory. Everything He does is motivated by the appropriate act of glorifying Him. He does what He does to glorify His own name.

> *For mine own sake, even for mine own sake, will I do it: for how should my name be polluted? and I will not give my glory unto another.* – Isaiah 48:11, KJV

We see thus far how God pursued and clearly stated to the children of Israel that they should worship Him alone. But we should look at Ephesians chapter 1 just in case we think that this is only pertinent to the Old Testament era.

The Apostle Paul wrote to the church of Ephesus and in his audience are both Gentile and Jewish believers. It is very apparent that Paul believes God saved us for Himself. God married us for Himself. After all, what man would marry a woman only for her to take off her wedding gown and the wedding band and then run off with other men while she still bears his name? None. So, God called us, washed us, and married us — gave us His name — for Himself. Therefore, He wants it all.

I believe, for emphasis, Paul, in Ephesians 1:5, 11, 13, and 14 (NLT), stated four times that God saved us from sin for Himself.

> God decided in advance to <u>adopt us into his own family</u> by bringing us to himself through Jesus Christ. This is what he wanted to do, and it gave him great pleasure. — Ephesians 1:5, emphasis added

> Furthermore, because we are united with Christ, we have received an inheritance from God, for <u>he chose us in advance</u>, and he makes everything work out according to his plan. — Ephesians 1:11, emphasis added

And now you Gentiles have also heard the truth, the Good News that God saves you. And when you believed in Christ, <u>he identified you as his own</u> by giving you the Holy Spirit, whom he promised long ago. — Ephesians 1:13, emphasis added

The Spirit is God's guarantee that he will give us the inheritance he promised and that <u>he has purchased us to be his own people</u>. He did this so we would praise and glorify him. – Ephesians 1:14, emphasis added

God intends to be praised and gloried in everything He does. Unequivocally, He deserves and should receive all praise and glory, and we are the main conduits through which such love and adoration should come. We are responsible for propagating the praise of God throughout the earth. With our good works, we should incite others to praise Him (Matthew 5:17).

Total Commitment

God purchased us to be His own with the precious blood of His Son Jesus Christ. When Jesus had completed all He came to earth to do on the cross, He said, *"'It is finished!' Then he bowed his head and gave up his spirit"* (John 19:30, NLT). This meant the work He came to earth to do was done. The price to redeem man back to His Father was fully paid.

Full ownership of something only occurs when a person fully pays for whatever it is that they are buying. This happens when there is no remaining balance on the item. This is the case with us. God, our Father, paid full price and brought us back from the claws of death and hell due to sin. Therefore, He owns us, thus He has the right to want nothing less than all of us.

Total dedication to God is not the same as commitment to church and its associated religious ceremonies, logistics, and activities. Dedication to God is nothing less than full commitment to the Person, Jesus Christ. We are to love God first. We are to connect ourselves to and abide in the Vine, and then service will flow from Him through us.

Those who have put church over God are seeking to work the ministry void of an intimate connection to and a life that is hidden in Christ Jesus. That will not work because that is not the formula that is set forth by the systems of heaven. Although church or ministry activities are good, we must love and want God first. We must want to encounter the Person, Jesus Christ. We must seek and find the Giver first and then the gifts will follow.

This encounter with Him will show in our conduct, and it will show in who we are in public and, more so, who are in private. As well, it will show in our personal integrity, in our loyalty to home, family, and community, and of course to the church.

When totally committed to God, we make Jesus our sole authority, our guiding light, and our infallible compass. Being committed to Christ means we move Jesus from being solely our Savior to our Lord *and* Savior. As our Savior, we declare Him as the one who brought us from a life of sin into fellowship with Him, that's it. Him being our Savior does not mean He is our Lord. All regenerated souls can say Jesus is their Savior, but not everyone can say He is their Lord. The book of Romans starts with these words: "*Paul, a bond-servant of Jesus Christ*" (Romans 1:1). A bondservant is translated from "*doulos*," which literally means "slave." Slaves have no rights; they do whatever the master says to do. That should be the perfect description of the nature of our relationship with Christ.

Dictionary.com defines lord as "someone or something having power, authority, or influence; a master or ruler." Lords have rulership or authority over their servants. So, we must have the mindset of being a servant to Jesus and only then will He be our Lord. Servants obey their master; they have no will of their own. This is why total surrender is unnegotiable for a follower of Christ. As the master of our lives, He wants and should have all of us, nothing withheld, nothing reserved, and nothing covered. He must have ultimate power and authority over our lives.

In giving all to Jesus and making Him the Lord of our lives, we surrender as slaves to His will. The key word here is surrender. None of this is against our will.

We serve as slaves or servants because of the love of Christ that draws us to Him. Jesus, our Master and Lord, is not like earthly masters. We are not held against our will, we are treated like sons and daughters, we are joint heirs with Jesus, and we have a remarkable reward awaiting us. Normally, slaves are not rewarded, and neither do they have rights to anything the master owns, but we are joint heirs with His Son Jesus. This is a great and incomparable blessing.

The other joyous fact about us being slaves to Christ is that we can abort the slave-master relationship at any time, but because this good Master is so loving and kind, we choose to stay, and therefore, we serve Him with gladness. This slave-master relationship is like none other. No other relationship is marked by new mercies every morning, provisions for the slaves' needs that far exceed what we ask for or think of, immediate pardon when we do wrong and ask for forgiveness, peace even when everything is falling apart around us, access to the Master, being able to talk to Him at any time, and the list can go on.

In this relationship of total commitment, we no longer live for our own gain, but instead, we allow Christ to live through us. Our motto then becomes, "Not my will but thine be done" and "None of me and all of You." Our greatest desire becomes, "I must die, and Christ must live." Galatians 2:20 (KJV) should become real to us:

I am crucified with Christ: nevertheless I live; yet not I, but Christ liveth in me: and the life which I now live in the flesh I live by the faith of the Son of God, who loved me, and gave himself for me.

A very important element to note, if we give all to God, is that we must die; self must be slain. Our anthem should be simple and concise: "*For me to live is Christ, and to die is gain*" (Philippians 1:21, KJV). We must give up our rights and ways and allow Christ to rule. We live with Christ in the flesh but not according to our will. Our will dies and the will of Christ for us comes to life in us. We allow Jesus and His Word to have the final say in all areas and affairs of our lives. We make Him king, ruler, and dictator of our lives. That is where He belongs in our lives. Yes, He wants it all. He wants to wipe the canvas of our lives clean and rewrite our lives for His glory.

When we give Him all, the chances of choosing church over God is not likely, neither is it likely that we will decline spiritually because we cannot go in a church building for church services and ministry activities. This will not happen, because in giving Him all, we are in a vibrant relationship with Him.

A Spiritual Health Check

Regrettably, there are a host of other masters in the lives of many Christians, masters that we place above the rulership of Christ. But we must remember that

Jesus must be the only master. He is not willing to co-rule with any other master. Jesus as Lord means that Jesus is the one and only supreme ruler and master in our lives.

Mostly, our dear brothers and sisters in Christ fall under the rule of a master other than the Lord Jesus because they acknowledge Jesus as their Savior, but not as their Lord. This is a primary reason why one would choose church over God or decline spiritually, simply because they cannot go in a church building. Too many in the church have misaligned priorities and are holding on to and chasing after things that have no real importance in life, especially our spiritual wellbeing.

For these individuals, the extra time on hand during the shutdown only afforded more time to fatten their idols. If social media, entertainment, your children, your spouse, working out, or any form of self-indulgence is your idol, that is where you would spend the extra time you earned from not traveling to and from work or church, for example.

Similarly, the money you saved by not buying gas or going into stores only to purchase items you do not need and did not plan on purchasing would be spent on your idols. How many believers subscribed to Netflix or any other entertainment network during the shutdown? How many over-indulged on food, movies, or video games? How many made no deliberate effort to use the extra time available to them to lengthen and deepen their time spent in prayer or in the Word?

Those who have placed church over God will not likely be proactive in their personal walk with God. These are the Supplanters, the Minimals, and the Church Lifers. In fact, the Church Lifers, particularly, could not function well during the shutdown. They probably were like fish out of water when they could not go in a church to worship, and we know what happens to fish when we take them out of water.

But if you are a Relational, you have chosen God over church, and you have made Him the Lord and Master of your live, meaning no foreign god has taken His place. You have a relationship with Him, not the good institution called ministry or church. Therefore, your lifestyle, well before the shutdown, is to guard your heart, spend time with Him, and pay moment by moment attention to your relationship with Him. You enjoy spending time with Him, in essence, you do the needful to keep a thriving and intimate relationship with Him. Therefore, during the shutdown, your disciplines in this faith-walk were already established. You have a deep desire for Him, the discipline to pursue Him, and you have delight in being with Him. That made it quite easy and natural for you to use the extra time and resources available to you for your spiritual enrichment and that of others.

A measure of the COVID-19 test: church or God is where we stand spiritually after the ban on corporate worship ended. Some questions to consider are:

- Were you eager to return to church after the ban on congregate worship was lifted?
- Did you wish the restriction on corporate worship had continued?
- Have you gone to church since churches have reconvened?
- Has your connection to church strengthened or weakened since the restriction on corporate worship?
- Did you struggle to find spiritually enriching things to do during the shutdown?
- Did you lose interest or did your interest in spiritual things decline during the shutdown?
- Did you feel out of place because you couldn't go to church?
- Has your prayer life improved since the ban on corporate worship?
- Has your discipline and regularity in reading the Word improved since the ban on corporate worship?
- Compared to where you were before the ban on corporate worship, are you closer to the Lord now?

- Compared to where you were before the ban on corporate worship, do you have a stronger prayer life now?
- Compared to where you were before the ban on corporate worship, would you say you are more on fire for God now?
- In general, did you spend most of your free time and resources during the shutdown due to the COVID-19 pandemic on yourself, others, your spiritual enrichment, or the spiritual enrichment of others?

We need to see ourselves in this picture. All believers made a personal commitment to Christ at one point in our lives. Many of us were zealous and on fire for God; we were hungry for spiritual things — Bible study, prayer meetings, worship services, cell groups, fasting — but then life happened. We now fail to pay close attention to the marriage. Our awe of Jesus, our lover, weakened and that opened the doors of our hearts for other lovers to get our attention, so the marriage deteriorated. But despite your affections being set on other lovers, you are still associated with the church — you have now chosen church over God.

Another scenario: you started a career and a family. Oh yes! You got married and your spouse comes first. This is a big trap. You had bills to pay and other demands on your time, so you had to work long hours. Perhaps you had more than one job which took time away from attending church and your personal prayer and Bible reading time. All of this is called life, and life happens to all of us. But our relationship with the Lord should not drift into the background and life should not take the foreground. If this is the case, life has taken God's place, making it your idol, and you have chosen church over God.

You have chosen church over God because although you still attend church and may be involved with a ministry or two, church is a minor part of your life, it is no longer a priority. You rationalize your backslidden state by telling yourself that you don't have time to serve as you used to. You have not openly rebelled against God, you are not living a sinful life, but you have drifted from your lover, the Lord. Your heart is in a different place. Your affections are elsewhere. Primarily, you spend your time, talent, and treasures on other things. You have put your house, your life, and your affairs above God. Like the church of Ephesus, you have left your first love.

This precarious spiritual position is a recipe for spiritual disaster during the shutdown, but all is not lost. Your loving Father is calling you back into sweet fellowship with Him today. Like a spouse who does not want to share his or her spouse with another, God does not want you to share your loyalty with another. He wants you back and He wants all of you.

One day you made a vow to the Lord, you made Him your spouse, and you married Him. You cannot just go out and do whatever you want with no thought for your spouse. You cannot put anything above your spouse and expect the marriage to be healthy. You cannot go and be with other men or women, and you cannot devote yourself to other people or things without causing problems in the marriage relationship. It is called spiritual adultery.

The covenant relationship will deteriorate if we love anything or anyone more than God. This is why Jesus asked Peter, not once, but three times if he loved fishing more than Him (John 21:15). Fishing was Peter's career. Fishing put a roof over his head and food on his table, but Jesus made it clear to Peter that he must love Him, Jesus, the Source (the Giver) more than he loves the resource (the gift). Could God be saying the same thing today about the job you have placed above Him?

God's Faithfulness to His Bride

The sustained commitment of both parties is a must for any covenant relationship to last. Both parties are responsible for the health and wellbeing of the relationship. In a spiritual marriage, we have the blessed assurance that our spouse will be faithful always. There's no doubt that God will do His part. He will never let us down or break His covenant with us.

When our spiritual marriages wane, it is always due to our own behaviors — the wondering of our hearts to other gods. It is never God that breaks His vow. Our relationship with God will thrive when we choose God over church and set ourselves apart for God, forsaking all others, and keeping ourselves only for Him. When we put everyone and everything — even good things, like ministry activities, church life, family, and work — that tries to distract us from loving the Person, Jesus Christ, and from loving God Himself second to none, our relationship with God will thrive. We must love God, the Person — not the things associated with God — with all our heart, soul, and mind (Matthew 22:37).

The price that was paid to redeem us from sin and give us access to God the Father was the highest there is. Jesus, the King of kings, was beaten beyond recognition, He was hung on a cross to die, and then placed in a borrowed grave. He did this for you and me. All of this was to redeem us from sin. As Jesus was fully surrendered to His Father all the way to Calvary, He asks the same of us: total and complete surrender, nothing less.

Out of gratitude to God for His love and mercy toward us, we should be completely devoted to loving Him, obeying His Word, and living according to His purposes for our lives.

Make the commitment today. Get back to your first love. Love Him for who He is, not for what He can do or for what He has done. Love Him, not the things that are associated with Him, not church life, not ministries, not good deeds! Love Him. Make Him the true lord and king of your life. Do not fall prey to the subtle tactics of the enemy by settling for good or even best in place of the superior. Idols of all sorts are less than superior. Make God your God.

PRE/POST COVID-19 SPIRITUALITY ASSESSMENT

To determine if you are a Relational, Church Lifer, Supplanter, or Minimal, choose the response option to each item that describes you best. Answer all questions and follow the instructions at the end of the assessment to determine your score and percentage and the group in which you fit best.

<u>**True**</u> (This is how I am most of the time. / This is an accurate description of me.) = 1 point

<u>**Sort of true**</u> (This is more true of me than false.) = 2 points

<u>**Sort of false**</u> (This is more false of me than true.) = 3 points

<u>**False**</u> (This is not how I am. / This is not an accurate description of me.) = 4 points

1. I wish the restriction on corporate worship had continued.	
2. I feel guilty when I miss a church service or event.	
3. I find that I have little to no interest in going to church since churches have reconvened.	
4. I struggled to find spiritually enriching things to do during the shutdown.	
5. I felt out of place during the shutdown because I couldn't go to church.	
6. I lost interest entirely in spiritual things during the shutdown.	
7. My interest in spiritual things declined during the shutdown.	
8. My prayer life improved during the ban on corporate worship.	
9. My discipline and regularity in reading the Word improved during the ban on corporate worship.	
10. I read inspirational books regularly, even before the shutdown.	
11. Compared to how I felt before the shutdown I felt further from God when churches returned to corporate worship.	

12. Compared to how I felt before the shutdown, I am more on fire for God now.	
13. I don't feel like I'm in good standing with the Lord if I'm not deeply involved with church ministries.	
14. When churches were closed because of COVID-19, I attended virtual church services at the same rate or more frequently than I attended in-person services before the restriction was enforced.	
15. Generally, I do not read my Bible during the week.	
16. I do personal fasts for my own spiritual growth and development.	
17. I fellowship with other believers – in church services, small groups, Bible studies, etc. – as often as I can.	
18. I do not attend church regularly. I go when I can.	
19. I attend weekly church services regularly, but I don't usually do much of anything during the week to build me up spiritually.	
20. I find it difficult to maintain my relationship with God or grow in Him when I can't go to church.	

Scoring Instructions

Each group has a maximum score — Relationals: 52, Church Lifers: 36, Supplanters: 36, and Minimals: 44. Total your responses for the items specified for each group and calculate the percentage of the maximum score. For example, if your total score for Relationals is 46, you would then calculate the percentage for 46 of 52 (46/52 x 100), which would be 88%. The group for which you have the highest percentage is the group in which you fit best.

<u>Relational</u>: Total the responses you selected for items 1, 2, 3, 4, 5, 6, 7, 11, 13, 15, 18, 19, and 20 and calculate the percentage of the maximum score.

Maximum score: 52

My score: _____.

My percentage: _____.

<u>Church Lifer</u>: Total the responses you selected for items 1, 3, 6, 8, 9, 12, 18, 19, and 20 and calculate the percentage of the maximum score.

Maximum score: 36

My score: _____.

My percentage: _____.

<u>Supplanter</u>: Total the responses you selected for items 8, 9, 10, 12, 13, 14, 16, 17, and 18 and calculate the percentage of the maximum score.

Maximum score: 36

My score: _____.

My percentage: _____.

<u>Minimal</u>: Total the responses you selected for items 2, 5, 8, 9, 10, 11, 12, 13, 14, 16, and 17 and calculate the percentage of the maximum score.

Maximum score: 44

My score: _____.

My percentage: _____.

Description of the Groups

Relationals are involved with church ministries and have a balanced life, including a dynamic and thriving personal relationship with the Lord that is marked by a disciplined and delightful prayer, Word study, and worship life.

Church Lifers are deeply involved in church life or church ministries that mainly define their faith-walk.

Supplanters replace personal spiritual enrichment activities such as a disciplined prayer, Word study, and worship life with weekly church services.

Minimals attend church intermittently, are marginally involved with church ministries, and do not engage in spiritually enriching activities outside of church.

I pray you found this book a blessing and that what you read will propel you into a deeper relationship with God.

Please consider leaving an honest review of the book on Amazon or Barnes & Noble.

Thank you in advance.

OTHER BOOKS BY THE AUTHOR

1. *The High Call of Forgiveness. It's A Mandate*
2. *The High Call of Forgiveness. Leader Guide*
3. *The High Call of Forgiveness. Student Workbook*
4. *The Self-Scarred Church*

FIND AND FOLLOW ME AT:

- Email: info@booksbyrosemarie.com
- Website: www.booksbyrosemarie.com. Subscribe to receive free resources, early notifications on new publications, weekly blogs, and more.
- Facebook: BooksbyRosemarie
- Twitter: @BooksRosemarie
- Instagram: books-by-rosemarie

END NOTES

[1] Bryson, J. R., Andres, L., & Davies, A. (2020). Covid-19 and rapid adoption and improvisation of online teaching: Curating resources for extensive versus intensive online learning experiences. Journal of Geography in Higher Education, 10, 1–16[1]

[2] Swift, C. (2020). Being there, virtually being there, being absent: Chaplaincy in social care during the COVID-19 pandemic. Health and Social Care Chaplaincy, 8(2), 154–164

[3] Parish, H. (2020). The absence of presence and the presence of absence: Social distancing, sacraments, and the virtual religious community during the COVID-19 pandemic. Religions, 11(6), 276. https://doi.org/10.3390/rel11060276

[4] Annabella Osei-Tutu, Abraham Kenin, Adjeiwa Akosua Affram, Akua Amponsah Kusi, Glenn Adams & Vivian A. Dzokoto. Ban of Religious Gatherings during the COVID-19 Pandemic: Impact on Christian Church Leaders' Wellbeing in Ghana. Pastoral Psychology (2021)

[5] Annabella Osei-Tutu, Abraham Kenin, Adjeiwa Akosua Affram, Akua Amponsah Kusi, Glenn Adams & Vivian A. Dzokoto. Ban of Religious Gatherings during the COVID-19 Pandemic: Impact on Christian

Church Leaders' Wellbeing in Ghana. Pastoral Psychology (2021)

[6] Five Things We've Learned During the COVID-19 Crisis. Articles State of the Church 2020 in State of the Church 2020 • May 13, 2020. https://www.barna.com/research/things-we-learned/

[7] O'Rourke, J. J. F., Tallman, B. A., & Altmaier, E. M. (2008). Measuring post-traumatic changes in spirituality/religiosity. Mental Health, Religion & Culture, 11(7), 719-728

[8] Han, J., & Lee, C. (2004). Ministry demand and stress among Korean American religious leaders: A brief report. Pastoral Psychology, 52, 473-478. https://doi.org/10.1023/B:PASP.0000031525.27365 .0c

[9] Lee, C. (2007). Patterns of stress and support among Adventist clergy: Do religious leaders and their spouses differ? Pastoral Psychology, 55, 761-771. https://doi.org/10.1007/s11089-007-0086-x

[10] Parish, H. (2020). The absence of presence and the presence of absence: Social distancing, sacraments, and the virtual religious community during the COVID-19 pandemic. Religions, 11(6), 276. https://doi.org/10.3390/rel11060276

[11] Miles, A., & Proeschold-Bell, R. (2013). Overcoming the challenges of pastoral work? Peer support groups and psychological distress among United Methodist church clergy. Sociology of Religion, 74(2), 199-226

[12] Han, J., & Lee, C. (2004). Ministry demand and stress among Korean American religious leaders: A brief report. Pastoral Psychology, 52, 473–478. https://doi.org/10.1023/B:PASP.0000031525.27365.0c

[13] Lee, C. (2007). Patterns of stress and support among Adventist clergy: Do religious leaders and their spouses differ? Pastoral Psychology, 55, 761–771. https://doi.org/10.1007/s11089-007-0086-x

[14] TOZER DEVOTIONAL. We Were Made to Worship. Fri, April 16, 2021. http://www.cmalliance.org/devotions/tozer?id=679

[15] One in Three Practicing Christians Has Stopped Attending Church During COVID-19. Articles State of the Church 2020 in Faith & Christianity in State of the Church 2020. July 8, 2020. https://www.barna.com/research/year-in-review-2020/)

[16] Millennials Are Leaving Religion And Not Coming Back, by Daniel Cox and Amelia Thomson-DeVeaux. December 12, 2019. Filed under Religion. https://fivethirtyeight.com/features/millennials-are-leaving-religion-and-not-coming-back/

[17] https://techjury.net/blog/time-spent-on-social-media/

[18] *God and Marriage*, p. 43

Made in the USA
Middletown, DE
09 June 2022